ON THE WAY HOME

An honest look into the heart of grief

BY TERRI DeVRIES

Holy Bible verses were taken from the New International Version (NIV).

Cover Art by Kelly O'Dell Stanley/KOS Design
Formatting by J.R. Roper/Hidden Cottage Press

Dedication

To Mel, whose loss is still incomprehensible, and whose view from heaven must be breathtaking. I wish there had been more time. We miss you every day.

Table of Contents

Introduction

Catastrophic loss can be equated with losing a home, bankruptcy, being fired from a job shortly before retirement age, or a debilitating illness. But for some of us it is death, the shattering loss of someone we love. It's as if a volcano erupted, spilling lava all over the landscape of our lives, eradicating our dreams for the future. The red-hot flow destroys our plans, changing the beauty of vibrant green hope into the dull, nondescript gray of despair, all hope laid out flat like matchstick trees on the mountainside.

Nothing about the landscape remains the same. We find ourselves in a world of grief, a world in which death has destroyed all it touches, leaving rubble in its wake. The vacuum of grief is a cold, dark, seemingly hopeless place. We are left with a depth of sadness we cannot describe.

For me (and perhaps you) the devastation was instant, my life altered in mere moments. Regardless of whether loss is sudden or gradual, the damage is done. It is painful. Irreversible. Inevitable. Irreparable. And for a time, all hope seems to be lost, joy stripped from life, and the word 'normal' deleted from the dictionary. I know it felt that way for me.

The necessary shock accompanying death is a blessing, insulating us from the intense pain of loss. Over time, as the shock lessens, pain will begin to insinuate itself into our lives, a gradual seeping in of our new reality. In small increments, we are forced to reckon with what happened to us.

Here's a hard truth; it's incredibly painful to own our grief. It overtakes our body and mind emotionally, socially, spiritually, and physically. All-consuming, grief fills every atom of our being, leaving room for nothing else. That said, though, it's necessary to grieve well, whatever that looks like for each of us.

However grief comes to you, allow yourself the pain. Allow the tears, the anger, the sadness. These are the ways you honor the one you've lost. Grieve alone in your home or your car, or with family members and close friends—when, where and with whom doesn't matter. It may happen soon after the loss, or take weeks or months. There is no time frame. The important thing is that you allow grief to come out when it feels right. You'll know.

I pray my story will in some small way help you along your journey through this thing called grief. Sometimes you just need to hear that someone else sees and understands.

I remember him

In the early morning sunrise and the red glow of sunset
In the burnished gold of fall and the white purity of winter

I remember him
In the green of grass and the purple of lupine
In the quiet of evening and the busyness of commerce

I remember him
In the tenderness of an old saint and the beating of a baby's heart
In the voices of my sons and the soft heart of my daughter

When I am filled with grief and shed quiet tears
When I see the gentle rain and hear the voice of thunder
I remember him

When I see a leaf and watch it fly on wings of the wind
When I hear the waves crash in and out on the lakeshore
I remember him

In each day, in each season, in each decade
The peace of it covers me and shields my tender heart
Gracing me with remembering

Prologue

We wept when we were born, though all
around us smiled. So shall we smile when we die,
though all around us weep.

—CHARLES SPURGEON

This Saint Patrick's Sunday morning we awaken to a gorgeous, sunny day. The evidence of spring is everywhere in the neighborhood. Bulbs are poking through the dirt, crocuses a riot of purple and yellow along our driveway. Looking out to our back yard as I sip my first cup of coffee, I realize how much I love everything about this season—the new green of grass and leaves and the fresh scent only evident in early spring.

As we drive to church, Mel remarks how similar this day is to last year's St. Patrick's Day when we were invited to our friends' home for a cookout to celebrate their new deck. We think it might be great to grill on our own deck tonight.

We return from the worship service shortly before noon, enjoy a light lunch, and settle in with the Sunday *Press*. As the temperature rises, I decide I might sit outside later on. After a while, Mel becomes restless and leaves the room. He reappears, dressed in his black compression clothes, topped with a tight-fitting hat.

"I'm going for a run," he announces. He's been talking about getting back into the routine of training for a marathon this fall–his third in four years—so this is no surprise.

"Have a good run," I say.

He heads out the door. A few seconds later he comes back holding up something brown. "Look," he says with a wide grin, "I found my scarf!" The scarf had been missing most of the winter, hidden on a hook in the garage beneath the under armour jacket he'd not worn since late fall.

"That's great," I say, and he leaves with a wave. Once he's gone, I sit back to finish reading the paper and play Words With Friends on my phone.

Forty-five minutes later I hear a siren across the back yard, absently wonder where it is, then go on with my game. We have our weekly Bible Study meeting at 4:30, so when Mel doesn't return in time to shower and change I decide either he's had a cramp (not unusual) and stopped to rest, or he's chatting with someone and lost track of time. At four-fifteen, I call our study host Lorilee to say we will be late because Mel isn't home. She tells me to call her when he's back. Though I don't let on to Lor, I'm worried enough to get into my car and look for him.

He is nowhere. I stop two runners along the way, ask if they've seen someone matching Mel's description. They haven't. As I drive, I can imagine him in the shower when I return home. He'll laugh at me for my alarm, tell me he took a new route because he was bored with the usual one. Of course that's what will happen, I tell myself, despite the niggling feeling in my subconscious that there is something. . . .

I've searched his favorite running routes in our neighborhood, and within twenty minutes I'm home again. He's not in the house. He's been gone far too long, but the phone hasn't rung. I've checked. Then I realize he has no identification on him—if something did happen no one would able to contact me. I take a breath and try to decide what I should do. The police? The hospital? I dial the hospital. As I wait for someone to answer, I think, *that siren a while back* . . . but no, it couldn't have anything to do with him.

The woman in Emergency takes my information, asks a few questions, puts me on hold. A man's voice comes on. A police officer. After asking specific questions *(was he wearing a wedding ring, what did it look like, what clothing was he wearing, was there another ring on his right hand, and might it have a black stone in it?)*, he says, "Ma'am, you need to come down." Though I press him to tell me what has happened, he repeats,

"Ma'am, please come down." And I know. My heart knows.

I begin to tremble, my heart pounding like it will leave my chest. What to do now? I know I can't drive, I'm far too shaky. My brain goes into autopilot, dictating logical steps. *Call Lorilee and ask her to drive me. Call Jeff (my son) and tell him to meet me at the hospital. Bring Mel's wallet with all his information.* I numbly pick up the phone to call Lor, who says she'll be right over. Then I call my son, who promises to meet me at Emergency. I'm shaking so hard I am barely able to speak, let alone hold on to the receiver. The world around me is shimmery, surreal.

The rest of the day is a nightmare. I vaguely remember Lor and our friend Jeanne driving me to the ER, Jeanne in the back seat, her hand on my shoulder. On the way she is praying aloud that everything will be okay, all of us knowing it probably won't be. At the hospital we are ushered into a small side room to the right of emergency arrivals, where the doctor gives us a rundown of what happened. A massive heart attack, no vital signs or blood pressure. All efforts to bring him back by emergency responders, ambulance personnel on site and ER doctors have failed.

Mel is gone. They did everything right, but now everything is wrong.

Jeff, his face chalk white, comes into the tiny, claustrophobic room. I can't say the words. I can't breathe. He knows by the look on my face, and starts to cry, this big, strong, youngest son, whose tender heart is breaking. We hug each other, unable to comprehend it all. *But I was with Dad yesterday—he helped me lay some tiles in my kitchen. . . .* He shakes his head, both of us unable to take it in.

Jeff and I are told we can see Mel now. I thank Lor and Jeanne for driving me, ask them to tell the group what happened, and they leave after hugs and promises of prayers. Then Jeff and I go to say our goodbyes to this man who has been a part of our lives for so many years.

Goodbyes.

For an hour we sit beside Mel's body, trying to wrap our minds around the truth. He is so cold, so still, the breathing apparatus left in his mouth, the knitted hat covering his head. We look at each other in disbelief, too shocked to do anything. Somewhere early in that hour I break the stillness, telling Jeff we need to call his brother and sister. He offers to make the calls, and leaves me alone with Mel.

This isn't real. *Please, God, tell me this isn't real.* I reach for his hand, his face, willing him to be warm, to sit up and say it's all been a joke. When I touch him his skin is like ice; all color drained from his face.

No, no, no. . . .

Jeff returns, his face suffused in anguish. They're both coming. They can't believe it. We are all enmeshed in a tight ball of shock. Our whole world has shifted.

The brown scarf Mel found earlier hangs in the garage.

1

Saying Goodbye

The presence of that absence is everywhere.

—Edna St. Vincent Millay

The first to arrive that night was my oldest son Marc who drove in from Milwaukee. He looked as shell-shocked as Jeff and I felt when he walked in the door. His fiancée Brittany would come as soon as she could, he told us. The two boys and I hugged and settled into the family room to await Michele and Ronn, who arrived from Chicago shortly before midnight. Michele explained they'd had to find someone to watch the kids; it was easier to keep them in school while we made the plans for visitation and the funeral. Ronn's dad and step-mom would bring them in a couple of days.

We huddled together, weeping, trying to make sense of everything. I don't remember much of the conversation that night. We couldn't wrap our minds around what had happened. Jeff went home to his wife and kids sometime after Michele and Ronn's arrival at midnight.

Exhausted from the events of the day and the long drives, the kids figured out sleeping accommodations and got sheets on the beds while I headed for my room. It was so strange, lying in bed alone, the words repeating over and over: *he's dead. He's gone. This is forever.* Wide awake, a video of the events of the day played in my head on a continuous track. Shock, disbelief, panic, a sense of disembodiment. . . . I was powerless to make it stop.

I felt compelled to sleep on Mel's side of the bed, his pile of clothes from earlier in the day in plain view, thrown on the chair as if awaiting his return. As if he would come back and wear them again. As if. His favorite red fleece, a pair of jeans, socks. Surely this was all a horrible dream.

The next day Marc, Michele, Jeff and I found ourselves seated in a semi-circle in the funeral director's office, a small, cozy room with a fireplace and comfortable seating reminiscent of a parlor in a Charlotte Bronte novel. We talked about arrangements. *Arrangements. Who came up with that word?*

Decisions had to be made, a long list of questions required answers. The funeral director sat beside his desk with a clipboard on his lap, ticking off each item we needed to cover. I deferred to my children, helpless to know what we should do. To their credit, they stepped up and steered me, helping me make decisions. I can't begin to express my relief and gratitude at the way they guided me.

Instead of following the norm, we planned a program meaningful and personal to us, one honoring to Mel. Each child took ownership of aspects of the service while I sat, numb in my grief, so thankful for each of them.

We spent two hours in that stuffy space, choosing, discussing, glancing at each other in disbelief and then getting on with the job at hand. Talking about Mel in the past tense was surreal. *He was, he did, he liked, he would have wanted.* The entire time I felt as if I were floating, present yet not really there.

Once decisions had been made and the time and date set for the visitation and service, we left the office and walked through the vestibule toward the front door. The smell of lilies permeated the building, the funeral smell, I remember thinking.

The following morning my children gathered pictures and chose several for the storyboards. I walked into the family room at one point and saw them sitting in a circle with photos strewn all around them, each with their choices from albums and boxes I gave them. Stories and laughter came out of those pictures—the remember-whens. What a precious memory as I look back.

Instead of having the funeral home take full charge, Marc and Jeff decided to make a video, while Michele designed and had the programs printed with photos and the format for the day of the funeral. Not only did those things cut a fair amount of expense, it also made for a more personal touch. We individually framed some of the poetry Mel had written, planning to place them on the tables for visitors to read as they waited in line.

We chose to do everything at my church in anticipation of a large crowd, a decision I am thankful we made. It was the perfect place. I will never forget arriving before visitation and seeing Mel's older brother, who came from New York, standing over the casket, tears streaming down his face. "How can it be?" he asked. I had no answer.

As expected, the line was endless at the visitation. We'd decided on one viewing for a three hour period and then another the hour before the service the next day. I couldn't have told you the names of the people who came other than siblings and family members. In addition to the numbness, I continued to suffer from sleep deprivation, my body so weary I found standing difficult as all those dear folks expressed their sympathy.

I stayed near the casket, glancing inside now and then to convince myself this was real, that it *was* him lying there. My youngest grandchildren were running around the large room, laughing and playing as small children should. Their childlike behavior lent an aura of normalcy, a rarity those days.

At one point I remember my four-year-old grandson coming to a stop before the casket to peer over the edge at his grandpa, unsure of what was happening. My son put his arm around the little boy as he knelt beside him, talking in a quiet voice while they looked at the body of this beloved man. I had to turn away, tears welling as three generations shared that moment. *Did Mel see it?*

I don't know how far beyond the three hours the line ran, but afterward exhaustion had so overtaken me I couldn't choke down the food someone provided for us. Bless all those thoughtful folks who cared for our physical needs, but what I needed was sleep, a good restful eight hours. It was a futile wish as I spent yet another fitful night.

We set the funeral for March 21, the 26th anniversary of the day my mother died. In the morning we were met with another endless line of people wanting to extend sympathy. After an hour the funeral director interrupted the stream of visitors, telling them they should go inside the sanctuary for the service. My family and I went into a separate room for last minute directions from the funeral home personnel and a few moments of prayer with my son-in-law, Ronn, and my nephew, Tony, both of whom are pastors and jointly conducted the service.

I have few memories of that morning, but I do remember being in the vestibule as we waited to be ushered in and seeing the sanctuary filled with friends from so many different parts of our lives. It instilled in me a sense of awe. All these people loved Mel, respected him, and had come to honor him. They came from Washington, Texas, Wisconsin, Illinois, Indiana, Colorado, Canada, Minnesota, New Jersey, New York and many parts of Michigan.

The boys put together a video, a stream of pictures set to music I had requested. The middle piece was one our oldest son, Marc, had composed and recorded. After the service, we had a dessert buffet to honor the fact that in heaven Mel no longer had to be gluten free—Celiac Disease had lost its hold on him. My youngest son, Jeff, had the idea, a celebration of Mel's freedom from earthly restraints.

It was perfect. He would have loved it. And I felt completely empty.

How long, O Lord? Will you forget me forever?
How long will you hide your face from me?
How long must I wrestle with my thoughts
and every day have sorrow in my heart?"

—PSALM 13:1, 2

2

The Reality Of Grief

Bereavement is what happens to you; grief is what you feel; mourning is what you do.

—Anonymous

Many psychologists refer to the process of grief as a journey. In some ways that's true—you are embarking on a trek that will take you through uncharted, unfamiliar and terrifying territory. There is no way of knowing how long you will take to get to the destination if, in fact, there is one; you only know the walk will prove painful, frightening, difficult and, at times, impossible. You will face roadblocks, detours, switchbacks, deterrents. It will be challenging, heartbreaking, discouraging, exhausting. But it will be necessary. The trail will sometimes disappear or be filled with obstacles. It will require every ounce of strength you possess to keep going. You must keep going.

Will grief end? Is there a sign somewhere saying you have arrived? I don't think so. However, at some point, the landscape around you begins to take shape. The shock surrounding you begins to wear down, allowing you to see outside its opaque walls. There, did you see the wildflower? If it bloomed before, you were incapable of noticing. Yet you see it now, and it's beautiful. You take a moment to lean over and smell the aroma. Did you catch a glimpse of the sunrise? It seems more vivid. The path has cleared enough for easier walking, the obstacles less menacing, farther apart. Your fatigue has lessened, seems more bearable. Your bouts of depression are longer between, not quite as harsh as they once were.

I will be on this journey for as long as I live. It ends when I join my husband in heaven, whenever that may be. I've learned many hard lessons so far. I often need to go backward for a while, like the switchbacks on the sides of the canyon in Utah's Canyonland National Park. You must go back to move forward. Back into the hard, raw grief, back into the gut-wrenching crying, back into the anger that threatens to tear you into ragged pieces.

There is something beautiful about grief. Our humanity comes to the surface and lies exposed, and we discover many people around us who see our pain, share in it and find ways to soften its sharp edges. In so many ways, big and small, they administer a balm to soothe our hurting souls. They cover us with a blanket of love and acceptance. They serve us a cup of cold water in the form of friendship, and they have no agenda, they need nothing in return, they demand nothing. In the worst of times, the best comes out in our real friends, and it's beautiful.

Those friends may not have experienced grief in their lives, at least not the kind you are walking through. It doesn't matter. They *see* your pain. In its perfect form, human kindness dictates walking alongside those who are hurting, sometimes in silence, sometimes with words; *I'm so sorry. I'm here. I love you. It's okay if you can't talk—we can just sit together.*

The landscape, so familiar all those days (weeks, months) ago is altered. Catastrophic loss does that— it takes on a life of its own. You feel as though your feet are in two different worlds; the one that once was and the one that now is, and neither is right. You long for the old, but it's gone. The new is unfamiliar, scary, and you can't summon the energy to adapt. Eventually, though, you must move your foot. You must choose the new world if you are to survive, and so you bravely do.

In the Bible, Jesus talks about having faith as small as a mustard seed, saying if you have that amount of faith you can move mountains. Grief is our mountain. Now the mandate is to figure out how our little mustard seed of courage can move our grief so that we can journey on. And that will take a lot of time and bravery on our part.

*Lord, help me walk with strength along
the path of grief. Give me the faith to trust that
you know the way, even on my darkest days.*

3

Reluctantly Solo

Whole years of joy glide unperceived away, while
sorrow counts the minutes as they pass.

—William Harvard

The endless stream of relish trays, meat and cheese trays, casserole dishes, and soups, each handed over with, "I don't need the container back," and, "You can freeze this for later," has begun. The cookies and breads, the case of wine, the flowers . . . I want none of it because I know what it means.

My husband of nearly 47 years died, and this is how friends show their love and concern, so I dutifully accept these gifts. But I don't want them. They represent a dreadful event, something I want with all my heart and soul to deny.

Maybe this is a dream, and I will awaken to find Mel here having his breakfast, or reading the Sunday Press, a *cup of steaming coffee in his hand. He'll wish me a good morning and hand me the puzzle page.*

I shake my head, willing it to be. Of course, my new reality has taken over and can't be denied. He's gone. Forever.

Nine days after Mel went home to heaven, the day was alternately cloudy, cold, rainy and snowy, sleeting and hailing. Then sunshine. The cycle repeated over and over. Heavy-hearted, I plodded through a hard day filled with "final" things to do, feeling so inadequate, so weary for lack of sleep. Even Ambien failed me. Yes, I was blessed to have my children and my family of friends who showered me with food, help, concern, prayers and visits. Abundant blessings, yet incredible pain. Yes, my church prayed for and supported me. Even so, I'd never been so lost or alone.

This experience had a learning curve—one lesson at a time on how to navigate uncharted territory. And one thing caught me by surprise; my anger, so much ANGER. Daily, I shook my fist at God. Why him? Why now? He was the picture of health. Trim, fit, and active. The youngest of five, each of his siblings had health issues and yet he was the one who died.

Why? I was beyond furious.

I wanted to scream at God. I *did* scream at God as I strode angrily through the house. So many older folks in bad health who wanted to go home and He had to take Mel? I demanded answers to questions with no answers. At least not on this earth.

It seems I am in good company. In the forward to C.S. Lewis's *A Grief Observed*, Madeleine L'Engle writes this:

I am grateful to Lewis for having the courage to yell, to doubt, to kick at God with angry violence. This is a part of healthy grief not often encouraged. It is helpful indeed that C.S. Lewis who has been such a successful apologist for Christianity should have the courage to admit doubt about what he has so superbly proclaimed. It gives us permission to admit our own doubts, our own angers and anguishes, and to know that they are part of the soul's growth.

I must admit, my owning the emotion did nothing to lessen it. Knowing others had similar reactions didn't make the pain go away, didn't stop the bleeding of my heart.

In some way, though, however small, it did validate the anger.

Then, to add insult to injury, in the midst of all the turmoil my vacuum died. The garage door opener stopped working. The garage light wouldn't go on. Ants invaded my pantry. My car battery died. And my chimney had had a recent fire and needed a new liner before I could use the fireplace again.

I hate this, I hate this, I hate this. None of it makes sense. None of it.

Then there were physical issues. First, a backache lasting far longer than usual. Next iritis erupted in one eye making it impossible to be in any light, so painful I needed sunglasses to watch television. Two weeks later I developed iritis in my other eye. It was an incessant parade of catastrophes. On top of all that, the income taxes were due to be filed, but the paperwork was far from ready. Had it not been so tragic, it would have been funny. *Really, God?*

The morning of the day my husband died, a song began to play in my head. When I awoke and for days afterward I heard the words on an endless track. I heard the song in the middle of a sleepless night and first thing in the morning. Over and over the refrain repeated.

"I know who goes before me, I know who stands behind. The God of angel armies is always by my side." ("God of Angel Armies," *Chris Tomlin*.)

One Sunday morning, a few months later, that song was chosen as an opening number at my church. As I stood and tried to sing, I had one of those "aha" moments. I had to stop singing as tears began to stream down my face. For months I'd felt alone, sometimes stranded due to snow, often solitary by choice. But was that true? I realized I'd had a traveling companion through these awful months. I didn't have to figure things out by myself.

God was trying to get my attention, to make me see He'd been there all along. My job was simple—I just had to let go of my anger and let Him guide me.

For he will command his angels concerning
you to guard you in all your ways.

—PSALM 91:11

4

Things That Go Bump
In The Night

*Fear: an unpleasant emotion caused by being
aware of danger: a feeling of being afraid.*

—Merriam-Webster

*I*n an attempt to keep a routine, I prepare for bed at eleven. I wash my face, smooth on lotion, floss and brush my teeth, take out my contact lenses and put on my glasses. It's a good routine, one which makes me feel grounded. This is what I do, have always done.

Our—no, my—room hasn't changed, except that I've moved to Mel's side of the bed, the side closest to the door. I feel more secure there, more comfortable. The TV is on, newscasters telling the news of the day. The weather forecaster informs me the next day will be sunny. After putting on my pajamas, I fluff my pillow and climb into bed. Beside me are my cell phone and a book. I check Facebook messages, set the timer on the TV, try to read for a few minutes, then turn off the light and settle in.

The only light in the room is that of the television screen. As I adjust to the darkened space, I hear a noise. My heart races as I imagine the cause of the sound. Is someone in the house? *Please God, don't let there be someone in the house. Keep me safe.* I'm too afraid to get out of bed; at the same time, I tell myself it's the best option. Check to verify no one is there. My imagination works overtime. Uncertain what to do, I do nothing. Eventually, I drift off to sleep.

At some point in the night, I hear it. Another noise. Again my heart pounds. Someone is there, in my doorway. The person comes toward me, speaks, though I don't understand the words. I'm terrified as the figure stands over me.

And then I wake up. It was so real, yet it was a dream. I breathe a sigh of relief, thankful. The thing is, I know it will happen again. Fear is becoming an all-too-constant companion, and I'm not happy. I want it to stop. *How do I make it stop?*

For weeks after Mel's death, this scene continued. I heard noises in the night; creaks, bumps, rattles. I dreamt someone was standing over my bed. Fear lingered, though I tried to reason with myself. My imagination is working overtime. Because I'm alone in the house, every little noise is magnified.

From the day I was born until several years into my marriage, I never spent a night alone. In later years when I did do so, it was only a night or two while Mel went on a business trip. I knew his absence was temporary on those rare occasions, and I don't remember having issues being alone.

Now things were different on so many levels. The fear came night after night. I spoke to a friend about the issue after a few weeks had passed. She told me of her experiences after her husband died, of having those same fears for a while. But eventually the fear went away. I've found that to be true for me as well.

Over time, I thought about it less. I've learned to accept the little noises in the night. The house might be settling, a branch brushing the window, a chipmunk scrabbling or a bird alighting on the downspout. Regardless, I'm sleeping better now, feeling more rested when I wake in the morning. The noises didn't go away; I learned they are part of life going on around me, even in the dark of night.

Accepting the sounds in the darkness, knowing them to be harmless—that is an accomplishment. It's all part of the adjustment you and I face on this solitary journey.

*So do not fear [anything], for I am
with you; do not be dismayed, for I am your God.
I will strengthen you and help you.*

—Isaiah 41:10

5

Honoring Your Loss

Lord, you have put me into this
role of widow with no warning, no goodbyes, no
instructions. Grief has wrapped itself around me.
Sometimes it chokes me and I can't breathe. I don't
understand. How do I do this?

My son-in-law, who is a pastor, stood at the front of the church at Mel's funeral, his eyes on the closed casket before him. The auditorium quieted as the people waited for him to begin speaking. He drew in a deep breath, looked up and over us all and said, "Death sucks."

Blunt, truthful words; he said what we all were thinking. Heads nodded throughout the sanctuary, and I was thankful for his honesty.

There is no upside to death for those of us left on earth, no replacement for the person we've lost. That's the reality.

If you are a person of faith, this is a difficult time for you. You may well turn away from God for a while. Or your loss might cause you to turn toward Him, but please note this; that doesn't always take the form of praise. Sometimes the turning toward comes in the form of anger, sometimes anguish, sometimes questioning, sometimes resignation. It's very hard in the midst of grief for it to look like praise.

Grief is powerful. It can wrench all the life out of you, leaving you unable to function.

Over the years I've read many books about grief. When my daughter was ten, her best friend, Shelly, died of leukemia after fighting for two long, painful years. The girls had been inseparable, more like sisters than friends. They spent many hours at our house or Shelly's, playing, drawing, sharing their hearts with each other. They had an underlying connection that went far beyond most friendships.

During the last months of her life, while Shelly went through chemo, surgeries and so much sickness in the hospital, I visited her twice a week; once with my daughter and once without. As time passed, I became increasingly angry at God. On many of my solo drives to the hospital I ranted at Him as I beat on the steering wheel. I witnessed the hospital staff's inability to relieve Shelly's immense suffering those last weeks, I saw the damage Shelly's illness did to my daughter, and my helplessness to *do anything* infuriated me. When she died that August, we all felt the impact of the loss. But here's the problem: I never actually dealt with Shelly's death.

My way of coping was to read. I read every book I could find on grief. I researched the term, spent hours at the library finding material related to grief—what it was, how to get through it, what to expect.

Most books and articles were clinical. Nearly all listed the 'stages' of grief, that be-all and end-all of lists; denial, anger, bargaining, depression, acceptance (Elisabeth Kubler-Ross, On Death and Dying). A tidy little package wrapped up in platitudes and rules and tied neatly with saccharine advice. In the end, I concluded, I would be done with grief and be able to move on nicely, *thank you very much.*

Unfortunately, that's not how things work. My method of dealing with it was to turn to the clinical aspect, to research and digest what the experts had to say. I didn't face the monster. I didn't allow myself to feel the grief. I did what psychologists call 'stuffing it.' Pushed it back into a room in my subconscious, locked the door and put away the key. All done. All better. And there it stayed for many years.

When my mother died several years later, I couldn't shed tears. I felt the loss, but didn't allow the grief to settle in, didn't let the tears wash some of the pain away. Maybe I was stoic; maybe I can't cry in public. The thing is, I didn't cry at all. Twenty years later, my father passed away. Again I didn't shed tears. It was as if the grief from all those years ago had taken away my ability to cry. I kept stuffing my sorrow into that locked room.

As I look back now, I see the groundwork God was laying for me, the preparations for this day in my life so many years later. There was much more I needed to do in dealing with this monster called grief, and when Mel died the lock finally came off, opening the door to that hidden room and allowing all the anguish to spill out.

The good news is grief serves a holy purpose. All the pain and brokenness you experience, each tear you shed, are a testament to the person you mourn. Grief honors your relationship with your husband, your wife, your parent, your child, your sibling or your dear friend. *Did you catch that? It honors them.* Grieving is evidence of their importance in your life. The remembering, the lessons they taught, the love shared with you, the permanent stamp on your life and that of your children and grandchildren—those things are the legacy left to you. Grief validates the person's value in your life. In its demented way, grief is good for us.

When I finally recognized that grieving was necessary and, in fact, healthy, my eyes were opened to

what I needed to do. There is no shame in crying, it ⹂
not a sign of weakness. It's God's way of allowing us to
wash away our pain a little at a time.

The ocean of tears I shed after Mel's death I shed
for all my losses, most especially the loss of my husband, but the grief covered much of the other losses
over my lifetime as well. I hope I've honored each of
those dear ones who have preceded me to heaven. They
are forever in my heart.

> *Precious in the sight of the Lord*
> *is the death of his saints.*
>
> —PSALM 116:15

6

It's All In The Details

*The best thing about the future is
that it only comes one day at a time.*

—Abraham Lincoln

I had no idea so many things needed doing right after
death. My daughter Michele stayed with me for two
weeks after Mel's funeral. During her stay, she assisted
with many of the details requiring immediate attention, help which was a real gift to me in my numb state.
Eventually, she had to return to Chicago to her young
family, and I was left to face my new reality.

My local funeral home helped in the area of
things that needed doing first. In the notebook they
gave me was a section titled "Next Steps." This segment contained information on contacting the SSA,
a checklist of things to do including changing names
on credit cards, bank accounts, financial accounts,

canceling Mel's driver's license, changing the titles of our cars and our house into my name, contacting insurance companies, etc. They also pointed me to an organization called Griefshare, which I will mention later in the book.

In those first weeks, I felt a need to find out the timeline of Mel's death. Morbid as it may seem, I needed to know. Maybe to help make sense of things, or maybe just to soothe my fear that he suffered. Whatever the reason, I called the hospital and asked for documents with any details they might have about those few hours before Mel died. They told me the fee for that information, which I paid in advance. The 16 pages I received told me nothing. There was no mention of who the doctors on call might have been, which ambulance service brought him in, or any clue of the timeline. When I called to ask more questions, the ER staff said they had no specifics to give me. How disheartening to wait for information giving me no answers to my questions.

About a month later a bill arrived in the mail. Life EMS Ambulance Service had charged a minimal fee for the services provided, but more important it gave me a place to go for the data I craved. I called the office which is not far from my home. The woman said they would be glad to give me anything they had as long as I proved my relationship and show Mel's death certificate.

I drove down that afternoon and was met by a sweet lady who gave me the documents she'd already printed out, and suggested I be seated on the nearby couch to read them through. If I had any questions, she would be happy to answer them. No charge for anything. Incredibly grateful, I sat and began to read. Most of the language was clear, every moment documented by a timeline and who did what. There were several pages, the last containing the time of arrival at the hospital.

I went to the desk to ask questions about a couple of the entries, and the lady called in a man, the head of the service. He took me into a small conference room, expressed his condolences, and went through the paperwork step by step, answering each of my questions. At the end, he invited me to call if any further questions came up, and asked if I had a support system, or if I would need suggestions of places offering grief therapy. I left with such a feeling of gratitude for that company. What an enormous difference between them and the response from the hospital. I now promote Life EMS in my area to everyone with whom I share my story.

There are no words to express the comfort I received from knowing how quickly first responders arrived after being called by the neighbor who saw Mel lying on the sidewalk. He was just a few blocks from home, almost directly across our back yard, when he collapsed. At first, I was afraid people would think me morbid for wanting those details, but in my heart I knew I could not rest until I had that timeline.

Reading the documentation of each moment from the time of arrival of the first responders and then the ambulance personnel, I knew every possible life-saving avenue was tried. I also knew that he died soon after the heart attack. That told me his suffering was minimal, another important bit of information which helped soothe my soul.

I'll never know the exact moment of Mel's death. The death certificate says 4:05, the time the hospital staff officially pronounced it, but the actual time was much closer to 3:10—moments before I heard the ambulance on that Sunday afternoon.

It may seem like a small thing, but I take comfort in knowing God took Mel quickly. He ran a good race, he kept the faith, and he won the prize. Praise God.

*I have fought the good fight, I have
finished the race, I have kept the faith.*

—II TIMOTHY 4:7

7

A Year Of Firsts

The last time I saw my husband he was running upward into the clouds. It was two weeks after he died, and I was at an Easter Sunday service.

Earlier in my adult life I looked forward to first times—first home after we married, first big trip, first child, first child to be married, first grandchild. Those were exciting events, things to anticipate. Never could I have imagined how I would dread the firsts of this coming year.

It began with Easter Sunday, two weeks after Mel died. I attended a beautiful service at a different church with my daughter Michele, feeling anything but joyful as my reality hit home. What was I there to do? Rejoice? That impossible concept swirled in my head. The last thing I wanted to do was *rejoice*. Sure, Jesus had risen, but what about my husband? He wasn't alive in my world anymore. *Would God strike me down for my cynicism?* Guilt consumed me for those thoughts, but my loss was incredibly raw. Mel had crossed the line between life and death, and he wasn't coming back. I was angry, tired, full of sorrow. We stood for the last song as the band played the intro to "Stronger" by Hillsong.

I mouthed the words on the screen, reading without comprehending. Until the bridge.

Then it appeared. I can't explain it in any logical way without sounding crazy, that vision beside the screen up front displaying the lyrics. Mel was running. In the split second I saw him he ascended, running up into a brightness that merged into clouds hiding what was beyond. It was so real.

It's the only time in my adult life I've had the sensation of seeing something so holy, and it started a shower of tears. I felt right being in that place, witnessing the gift I so needed then. My pain didn't lessen; it didn't solve any of the myriads of issues I would be facing over the next months. But I received a small taste of the peace I desperately sought. What a gift! And I breathed a prayer. *Thank you, Lord. He was one of your beloved saints, and I know you welcomed him with open arms.*

It seemed so impossible, so . . . strange, that I chose not to mention it to anyone for a long time afterward. But I got an odd sense of comfort. Whenever I hear the song now, I visualize what I saw that Easter Sunday.

Eventually, I returned to my church—alone. I won't sugar-coat it. It was hard. To this day, I stumble along, trying to walk into church with confidence, to be brave. To turn in the right places, to pause at the right times, choose the right things, say the right words.

In early April I called my oldest son, Marc to wish him a happy birthday. A hard call to make, knowing a piece of the picture was missing. I barely got the words out, wanting desperately to sound happy for his special day, but we both felt Mel's absence, both trying to keep the conversation normal—as if it ever could be again.

I dreaded all the firsts yet to come. So many of them; children's and grandchildren's birthdays; Mother's Day, Father's Day; our anniversary, his birthday, Thanksgiving, Christmas, my birthday….

Death comes with no instructions; no neat little packet marked 'Open upon death of a loved one.' It barrels toward you like a Mack truck, hits hard, and leaves you bruised, helpless to figure out how to make all those broken bits of yourself fit back together. It's messy; pieces are missing. And here's the question: how can anything ever be normal again?

I've said it before. Grief is a monster. It rears its ugly head every day, sinking its teeth in and causing excruciating pain, even in elusive sleep. My husband is *dead*. Just saying that ugly word out loud fails to make it real. Friends assure me time will heal, but at this moment, I am not a believer. What do they know? They haven't been there. I doubt the hole he left will ever be filled again.

On one particularly challenging day, physically and emotionally drained, I crumpled to the floor in tears, officially in the pit of hell. Feeling beaten and worn, unable to see hope in the future, I lay at the bottom of that dark chasm too exhausted and despairing to find a way out. *It's so lonely here. Desolate. Cold.*

I. Hate. This.

As I closed my eyes, about to surrender to the nothingness, I began to hear the words of a song we had chosen as the final one for the video at Mel's funeral, a shot of Mel crossing the finish line at his last marathon. *Oh, I'm running to your arms, I'm running to your arms. The riches of your grace will always be enough. Nothing compares to your embrace, Light of the world forever reign.*

And there it is. My reason to go on, to rise out of this pit I'm in. But here's the beautiful thing—I don't have to do this on my own. God will lift me up. All I have to do is ask.

He lifted me out of the slimy pit,
out of the mud and mire, he set my feet on a rock
and gave me a firm place to stand.

—Psalm 40:2

8

Home Sweet Home Alone

There is no way out—only a way forward.

—Michael Hollingsworth

I n April I go to *The Dells* with Ronn and Michele and *the kids to have some time away. I try to enjoy the water park, watching the kids swim and slide. They persuade me to go on a couple of the water slides with them, but most of the time I sit with an open, unread book and overlook the huge wonderland of water. I'm glad I came with this precious part of my family; I can feel their love for me. They are so sweet, trying to attend to my every need. Yet, all I want to do is go home.*

The reality hasn't hit me. Even though I saw Mel, or rather his body, saw there was no life, touched his cold hand, sat beside him for over an hour waiting for him to breathe, to sit up and tell me this was all a joke, it isn't real. How long before my heart accepts the truth?

I want to go home. I want healing, a sense of peace, a stop to the restlessness, a decent night's sleep. I want him back. I want to go home.

Yes, I was glad to get away for a while. And yet, when my daughter urged me to spend a few days at her house once we returned from the Dells, I had no desire to do so. I couldn't get home soon enough, all the while knowing nothing was waiting for me except an empty house filled with memories, echoes of a silenced voice, clothes that would go unworn, a second car without a driver, pictures of us from the past. I don't remember what my excuses were for leaving the moment we got back to her house. I was driven by a need to be home.

I cried most of the three-hour drive, angry tears, sad tears, pain-filled tears, broken-hearted tears. Never again would we take a family photo with him. Never again would he drive to work, or church, or whatever errand the day dictated. Never again would he come through the door asking what was for dinner. I knew the house would be empty. I knew I could have stayed away a month, and it wouldn't have mattered.

So why was I racing home?

There is in each of us a deep-seated need for feeling normal, especially in a time of trauma. When our normal is taken away, we tend to go where we feel safe, to a haven that gives us a sense of security. Like a child who runs to his mother when he is afraid or hurt, we run to our safe place, our refuge from the storms of life. That place for me was my home.

Only at home did I feel comfort. I craved solitude at my deepest level, needed to be where Mel had been, the place in which we spent the past 30 plus years enjoying the house I loved at first sight. The house we transformed a room at a time. The basement we finished with the help of our youngest son, Jeff, who was just beginning his own construction business. The yard we gutted and landscaped our way over a period of three years. The deck Mel and Jeff built together, one board at a time.

Here, I felt right. As I entered my house that day, I saw it with the eyes of one stepping into a new reality. I had no idea how the future would play out for me. Only three weeks had passed since Mel died, far too short a time for me to make any kind of major decisions, I knew that much. Looking back, I realize I was deep in the quagmire of shock, insulated from the coming pain. But I was home, the right place to be.

I understand so little of this process of grief, yet this I know for sure. The theory about stages is wrong. We bereaved don't reach acceptance. We don't recover from grief. If we are lucky and if we are strong, we simply learn how to live with it.

—ANDREA WARREN

9

Finding Faith

*In our darkest moments there
is a light within us waiting for the right time to
shine and guide our way.*

—UNKNOWN

The trim white houses stretch as far as I can see, clones set in a row like soldiers at attention. Each yard is manicured, each driveway an exact replica of the next. Identical mailboxes have no numbers to distinguish one from another. Panic overtakes me. Where is he? It seems as though I've been searching for hours.

I've knocked on dozens of doors and gotten no answer. I'm frantic. Not a soul is in sight—no children playing in the yards, no fathers mowing lawns or trimming hedges, not a single car on the road. Fear constricts my throat as I try to call his name, but I can't speak. The stillness is eerie. I hurry on, searching for him somewhere on this endless *street, searching, searching. Where is he?*

I awaken with a start, my heart pounding as my eyes dart around the room. I see the familiar tied-back curtains, the floral throw pillows on the chair. My heart begins to slow, panic recedes, and I tell myself it was just a dream. Slowly, I rise, pull on my robe. It's Saturday morning. The coffee will be on in the kitchen, the day ours to plan. Maybe pancakes will be started, Mel's famous, fluffy pancakes, the batter waiting for me to appear before he pours it onto the griddle.

But then reality dawns, and I'm forced to remember. That comfortable routine is forever gone. My husband isn't going to be there. Coffee won't be waiting for me. My normal will never be normal again, at least not in the old way.

I've been a Christian for as long as I can remember. My parents endured a cruel war in the Netherlands before they brought our family to America in search of a better life, and their first years here were hard. We had little money, but there was an abundance of love and an unshakeable faith. I remember my father whistling hymns as he worked in the fields, my mother singing, sometimes in Dutch, other times in English. I suppose you could say I inherited my faith. I didn't question God in those formative years. It didn't feel real then the way it does now, though. And I wonder if their faith grew out of the ravages of war, just as mine is growing out of the deepest grief I've ever experienced.

For a long time after Mel died, I seriously questioned my faith. As Christians, we have the audacity to think we can control our lives, that God needs our prayer notes on how He ought to change things when they aren't going our way. This, even though we were taught God has ultimate control. We know what our future should look like, and we waste no time in protesting if He chooses to alter the plan. After all, who knows better than we how the plan is best executed? I think God must laugh out loud sometimes when He hears our pathetic outcries. *No, God, that's not how I planned it. See, this is the way things should be.* As if I know better than He does. As if I have any say in what happens next. The hardest thing you and I can do is to let go of all that—all the control—and completely trust that He knows best.

When our tidy plan is ruined, when all our hopes are smashed, we morph into two-year-olds and throw a temper tantrum. We become angry and belligerent. A bad thing happened to us. It cuts deep, creates scars, and is excruciating. We can't find an end; we can't believe release will come at some point. All we know is this moment, this pain, this gut-wrenching agony that seems to be endless.

So yes, my faith was shaky in those weeks (months, more accurately) after Mel died. This thing called faith can be elusive. Where does it go in the deepest, most painful days of our lives? It's one of the hardest, most painful questions we can ask. How can faith exist in a world where death takes children, siblings, spouses, dear friends long before their time?

But then I think, *how can it not?* What do we have if we don't have faith? It is far too great a gift for us to shove aside, question, or ignore its importance. My grief tested my faith; I don't doubt that. In the process, though, I found my faith deepened as I felt the comforting arms of God around me in the middle of the night, or in the loneliness of the day. He knows grief. He watched His son die in agony on the cross. If He doesn't understand, then who does?

> *Blessed are those who mourn,*
> *for they will be comforted.*
>
> —MATTHEW 5:4

10

Discovering Joy

Like the parting of the clouds that lets a narrow
shaft of sun pass through, my ability to express
myself through words is beginning to return. It's a
welcome slice of normal, and I thank God for the
words that come. They release pain and point to a
brightness just beginning to peek over the horizon.
They signal hope. And just the tiniest bit of joy.

That first summer I spent a lot of my time outdoors. Growing up on a farm gave me an inborn
appreciation for nature; I love to watch things grow
and change, to enjoy the beauty of flowers and trees.
Because we had a small population of deer on our
property all year long, my husband and I didn't grow
a vegetable garden, but we did plant many deer-proof
flowering bushes and trees along with the perennials.

As I sat on my deck one day, I noticed a single

maple leaf quivering and shifting on the newly-sealed boards. A drop of rain from the previous night's shower shimmered as it glided off the edge of the leaf. I was mesmerized by the leaf as it lifted, floated for a second, and settled back into a new spot. It no longer had life, and yet it moved from place to place, carried by the wind.

How amazing, that little bit of motion caused by something invisible. I saw movement everywhere—each leaf, branch and seed pod swayed by the light wind. Raindrops rolled off, fell on my arm. Shadows danced with the sun, making an ever-changing, abstract pattern on the deck.

And I thought to myself, life is like that. Ever-changing, unpredictable. That's what makes it so beautiful; all those little surprises unveiled each day if only we stop and allow ourselves to see them. Yes, reality is harsh when the unexpected pain debilitates us. It's not just the good that makes life beautiful; it's also the pain, the bad that happens. At those times we can't see beyond *right now*, but out of the pain will come something salvageable and precious.

I'm not an advocate of pain. Pain is, well, painful. But I was born with my father's optimistic temperament, and I have to believe that out of my pain will come something beautiful. It may take a long time to discover, but I hold on to the hope that it will come, if for no other reason than to keep my sanity intact.

Right now I don't like this life I've been given. It's hard. There's so much anguish. I'm honestly trying to see around the negative. I (almost) believe it will get better.

That day as I watched a gust of wind pick up the leaf and blow it away, it struck me that in my current situation I am the one being carried by an invisible force. I need to remember all I have to be thankful for, so much joy to be felt for what I still have. You see, joy doesn't preclude pain, a lesson I've learned many times over. Joy is a state of mind.

I look forward to the day I get to the other side of grief, but in the meantime, a seed of joy remains. Life does go on, and despite the suffering we go through, we can still enjoy unexpected beauty.

My coping mechanism is to either sleep through the pain or make myself so busy that I can't think about it. Neither option works well over the long run. My pity party barred positive feelings for a long time until I understood that while I can't change my circumstances, I do have the power to identify the blessings given to me.

The struggle is ongoing, this positivity I'm trying to grasp. Relinquishing the control, learning to give thanks in all circumstances—those are hard things to do. And I admit it goes against my nature to let go.

But I'll keep trying. In the end, it will be worth the struggle.

*Now is your time of grief, but
I will see you again and you will rejoice, and no
one will take away your joy.*

—JOHN 16:22

11

Ceremony: A Way to Heal

When the funeral is over, it's not over.

—Angie Cartwright

The subject of final preparations and funerals never came up while my husband was alive. Mel and I avoided the topic: after all, we had years to make plans. How wrong we were.

As my kids and I discussed what to do for Mel, we each voiced a wish to be cremated. Since no directive was in place, we decided on cremation for him as well.

At a family meeting later, I asked my children where we should put a memorial for their father. A local cemetery was rejected, but each of us wanted a *place* we could go. I suggested Millenium Park, where Mel loved to run. A large, naturally wooded area of running paths winds throughout the park. Two lakes joined by a channel and covered with a beautiful bridge became our spot for a memorial.

I gained approval from the parks department to install a bench and large boulder on the side of the bridge facing the water. A contact of mine was able to work with a company which made a bronze plaque inscribed with Mel's photo and the wording we chose.

The next time we all gathered, we went to the park, taking pictures, admiring the scenery Mel had loved, and remembering him. Some of his ashes found their way under the boulder, making us feel closer to him at each visit.

During the summer I spent a weekend at Higgins Lake with a dear couple we were close to. The lake was one of Mel's favorite places in the world, out on the water watching the sunset and enjoying our time with friends. Just after sunset, we had a moment of quiet as I poured some of his ashes into the water.

Bittersweet moments, small ceremonies to honor him, those were a balm to my heart. I knew he loved Millenium Park, and I knew he loved the lake. Those marked times of healing for me.

Shortly after returning home from the lake I wrote the following.

come to rest

the moon moves above the edge of the
world where waters meet sky, peers

over the horizon
blood-red, gliding
lighting the single star standing guard

is that you watching the boat
cut silently through sharp
waves as I see where to spread you out?

a wispy cloud crosses moon's face
evaporates as
you embrace the lake

stretched

thin and reaching

heaven's gossamer film

12

It's A Big Deal

*The loss was difficult enough
to deal with. I wasn't expecting this sudden
change in "job description" too.*

—LORRAINE PETERSON, RESTORE MY SOUL

*nother week of firsts: cleaning some gutters, putting
the deck furniture in the storage shed, raking leaves
and using them to mulch the rose garden, taking care of
legal matters, cleaning the furnace filters...all by myself!
#feelingproud* (Facebook post, November 1, 2013)

Now, those of you who haven't walked through
grief may not understand why I would write such bor-
ing things on Facebook. They are mundane, ordinary
jobs, ones you might do on a regular basis. No big deal.

But it is. It is a huge deal to someone who may
want to crawl under an afghan on the couch and pass

the day burrowed under it. Considering that I could barely get myself dressed every day, those chores posed a massive challenge. I had to force myself out the door, order myself to get them done, and put one leaden foot in front of the other to do it.

I must say it was hard. Angry at Mel for leaving me with these jobs traditionally his, I spent a considerable amount of time telling him so. I was angry at God (and I told Him so, too) for taking Mel and forcing me to deal with extra responsibilities. And I was angry at myself for feeling inadequate in so many ways, and for tears because of added burdens and the crushing grief which beat me to a pulp. Most of all, I was angry at being sorry for myself.

For the past twenty or so years, my husband and I talked about what retirement would look like for us. We imagined doing some traveling, having time to putter around the house and yard, visit the grandkids more often. Personally, I hoped for more help in the daily chores and in the yard we had landscaped. I was expecting to do less work, not pile on more. Someone made the comment at one of my Griefshare meetings (which I'll tell you about in a later chapter) that she had less time for getting out because she had to do the work of two people.

It's true. My husband kept the garage clean, mowed the lawn, shoveled the snow, cleaned out the gutters several times a year, repaired things around the house, did a lot of the pruning, disposed of the weeds I pulled, washed the cars, did the taxes, and so much more. Now it's all up to me. I have decisions to make without his input, major purchases to decide on, yearly maintenance to schedule on the furnace, the air conditioner, the car. I have to put away the deck furniture in the fall and put it back again in spring; I have to take care of the leaves and branches that fall in autumn. It overwhelmed me.

I needed to affirm I *was* capable and strong enough to do what needed to be done, to be confident in my decision making. Never did I dream that I would be doing all this so early in my life. I'd planned another twenty years for the two of us to enjoy our lives.

Philippians 4:13 tells me *I can do everything through him who gives me strength*. I hope I can. I'm trying.

13

Oh The Lies We Tell

Listen (to me). It's the greatest compliment
you can give: that I am worth hearing.

—Dona Hoffman, Yes, Lord

The phone rings and I check to see if it's a robo call. I recognize the Chicago area code so I pick up the receiver.

"Hello, Michele." I continue unloading the dish-washer as I talk to my daughter.

"Hi, Mom. Just thought I'd check on you—I'm a little early picking up the kids at school, so I have a few minutes to talk. So, how are you?"

And the lies begin. "I'm fine. How about you?"

My son Jeff stops over with a warm hug (those precious and unexpected moments that mean the world to me) and asks a similar question. I give him a similar response, then ask about the kids. Why can't I just be honest?

Marc calls from Milwaukee. I love when he does this, and I think how fortunate I am to be so loved by my children. Again I answer I'm fine when he wants to know how I'm doing, and I inquire about Brittany. Notice how masterfully I deflect the spotlight off myself and onto my children? I'm a pro at this. I've been doing it for several months now, and I must say my technique is impeccable. Is it my pride that doesn't allow me to be honest? Or am I afraid of the truth?

At first, all those months ago, I craved space, needed my private time to come to terms with the impossible truth. I didn't communicate much and avoided questions as often as possible. When you do that, people eventually stop asking, and at some point they assume you're doing well. With my kids I was still in the evading phase.

Michele, Jeff and Marc weren't so easily fooled. They knew to ask key questions, and eventually I confessed to the actual state of my life. Bless them for asking.

At this point, I need to insert a word of caution. So much of the spotlight was on me. My kids tried to make sure I was doing well, had someone to talk to, had everything I needed. For a long time, I never thought *they* might not be doing so well. That *they* lost Mel too. That *they* had an open wound to deal with, grief that hit them fresh each time they walked into this house, and their dad wasn't here, or when I went to their house, and I was alone coming through the door without him.

I'm learning to be honest when the question comes up now. They want to know. I need them to know. But the reverse is also true. We've all lost this husband, this father, this grandfather, and those losses are different to each individual. We are all on this grief journey together. Be aware of *their* loss. Pay attention. Ask them the questions they've been asking you.

Take care of each other. Pain is pain. Loss is loss. However you shape it, whatever you color or name it, we've all witnessed the devastating effects. So make sure you acknowledge it. And support each other on this impossible journey.

Carry each other's burdens, and in this
way you will fulfill the law of Christ.

—GALATIANS 6:2

14

Facing The Waves

*To sail to the port of heaven we must sail some-
times with the wind and sometimes against it—
but we must sail, and not drift, nor be at anchor.*

—OLIVER WENDELL HOLMES

On a late August evening as I sat on the beach
in Grand Haven and watched the sun work its
magic on the western sky, I heard it. The silence. Rib-
bons of oranges, reds and pinks were interlaced across
the horizon as the sun descended beyond the edge
of Lake Michigan. It was our 47th anniversary, and I
had no idea how to celebrate alone. So I drove to the
beach to watch the sunset on our special day and sat,
cocooned in silence, the thunderous silence which had
surrounded me for the past six months.

I remember the roar of the water enveloping me
like a blanket, a comforting sound that helped drown

out the pain. The wind pushed the water onto the shore with relentless force. Yet even through the crashing waves I heard it—the silence.

I had no plan. That day on the beach watching the water permeate the sand, tears streaming down my cheeks, I felt like one of those pieces of shell being tossed up, swallowed and spit out on the shore over and over. Tossed and thrown at the will of the water, I could identify with their inability to escape the waves.

Several feet inland from the lake, a little boy had dug a hole in the sand and was sitting inside, pure delight on his face as he splashed the water seeping up from below the ground.

Seagulls flew low along the shoreline, squawking as if supervising the child's work. All those sounds of a lake at eventide—the crashing waves, the squawking seagulls, children squealing as they ran into the water—were powerless to drown out the silence.

As I watched the sun glide beyond the water's edge, I repeated the words I had said to my children on the day of my husband's funeral, words soaked in tears of my grief.

I don't know how to do this.

My fingers touched a small, smooth stone. Have you ever looked carefully at one of those stones on the shore? Admired how shiny they are, how the striations create a variance of color and nuance? Feel it in your palm—soft, silky. You find yourself carrying the stone down the beach as you walk, stroking the surface. You may even keep it as a souvenir of your walk.

How did the stone get so glossy? Think about it. A rock goes into the water as a sharp-edged, rough chunk of stone. Tossed about, thrown against the stationary boulders, shoved into the sand for eons. Gradually the edges begin to soften, the rough exterior smoothed. It's nature's rock tumbler. The nondescript outer layer is burnished away, leaving the colors and layers of pattern clear.

For me, this is a great analogy. My grief is that rock with all the sharp edges and rough coating. But just wait. In God's time it will be tossed, sanded and smoothed into something unique, priceless. The grief will become memories to cherish and keep in my heart.

I'm not there just yet, but I have friends who are. They are encouraging me to wait patiently for my time to come. I believe them. They are strong, God-fearing women who speak the truth. You and I may have some smoothing and polishing yet to be done, but we will come out beautiful and strong. Your time frame will vary from mine and those of my friends. That's okay, as long as we know where we're going.

That day on the beach as I watched those last rays of sun recede and surrender to the darkening of night, I knew it was time for me to go. I made my way back to the car, back to the abnormal silence of my home.

I don't think I'll ever get used to it. Walking into an empty house after dark, especially on a day meant to be celebrated by two, being alone seemed so . . . wrong.

After breakfast the next morning I picked up my cold cup of coffee to set it in the sink. The radio playing in the kitchen masked the silence of my empty house as I dumped the liquid and rinsed the cup.

And then I heard the song that had begun playing in my head the morning of that awful day. Chris Tomlin's 'God of Angel Armies.' I believe God placed the song in my head to help me through the following pain-filled days and weeks ahead.

And nothing formed against me shall stand
You hold the whole world in your hands
I'm holding on to Your promises
You are faithful, You are faithful.

Though I was carried back to that life-shattering day once again, this time I sensed something I was unaware of then. It was like warm, comforting arms around me, and now I know what it was. My God of angel armies had wrapped me in his arms, fulfilling his promises to me.

And surely I am with you always,
to the very end of the age.

—MATTHEW 28:20B

15

Happy Holidays

God will carry you through every storm
and give you the strength to make it.

—Anonymous

As I look out the window at the blowing snow and
remember the storms I'd faced these past few months,
this was a perfect message. God bless all those of you in the
midst of your own storms. Just know He's there, even if you
don't see Him.

On one December morning, I was preparing for
Christmas and thinking of the upcoming day with my
children and grandchildren. I knew how hard it would
to be for us all to celebrate without our husband, father,
grandfather there with us.

Everything needed doing before my December
work schedule began at a local retail store the two weeks
before Christmas. I figured working would be good for

me, especially this year, since the workdays were long and kept me physically and mentally occupied.

At home the decorations were up, the candles set in the fireplaces ready to light, my three kinds of Christmas bars made and stored in the freezer, the gifts purchased, wrapped, bowed and placed under the tree. I'd filled the stockings with chocolates and assorted trinkets for the kids. I'd taken Mel's Christmas ties and wrapped one for each of the adult boys, and for the girls I had framed a recent photo of Mel.

I was busy. I thought I would have no time to be maudlin once my schedule at the store began. And it worked.

Okay, fine, it worked for a while. . . .

Lord, this is so much harder than I ever could have imagined. Please show me the way.

aide memoire

this is all there is
a gathering of dust restored
to a prior state
a trace of scent dispelled

movies in 8 track
images framed on walls
situated on shelves
bonded to a boulder

this is all there is

days meld into nights
measured ticks
of all things passed
shadows carved in brass

this is all there is
a mask of cloisonné
the façade cloaking
residuals of remembrance

16

Blindsided

*Grief comes in and out like
waves from the ocean. Sometimes when you least
expect it, a huge wave comes along and pulls your
feet right out from under you.*

—Alan Wolfelt, Understanding Your Grief

That Sunday, three days before my first Christmas alone, I went to church in the morning. Snow had been falling all night, making the world worthy of a Currier and Ives painting. Had it not been for the cars on the road, I might have imagined myself back in that time, floating along the snow in a horse-drawn sleigh. It was so beautiful.

The church service was lovely. Glowing trees and wreaths and bright poinsettias adorned the sanctuary. As everyone bustled in, stamping snow from their boots and shivering as they removed their coats, people commented about the beauty of the day, so fitting for a Christmas celebration. Gradually the congregants filed into the sanctuary and took their seats. At the time of greeting each other I heard, "Blessed Christmas," "Blessings in the New Year," as warm handshakes were exchanged.

A sense of peace filled the room, filled me, and time slowed as we sang the songs of the season and heard an Advent message. The carols of Christmas held such hope and anticipation, assured the worshipers of God's love for us in the form of a tiny baby.

Peace.

I've always believed Christmas needs to have about it a pervasive sense of peace. A time to think about the young woman, a teenager at most, trusting the God who gave her the ultimate privilege of carrying His son. To think about this man, this carpenter who believed Mary when she told him of the angel's visit, her subsequent pregnancy, about his loyalty to his future wife. To think about this helpless infant, born in the dark of night in a stable filled with animals and straw. And to think of the Father, who sent a child to save the world He loved so much He was willing to sacrifice His only son. It's overwhelming, that ancient story.

The service, a time in a quiet place of safety and beauty, was the refreshing for which my soul longed. It was a beautiful hour of seasonal music, passages from the Bible telling the Christmas story, and a message of hope. Leaving the church building, I felt the peace previously denied me.

Then I went home, and it hit; my personal storm to match the growing snowstorm outside. It was to be a snowy day with much accumulation as the white flakes settled in a thick blanket on the lawn and flower beds outside my window—the kind of snow that kept most people indoors, at home.

Blindsided is the only word that describes what I felt. I sat down, awash in self-pity and wailed. The gut-wrenching agony stabbing through me was especially cruel that day as I sat in my family room, isolated from the world.

In his book, *A Grief Observed*, C.S. Lewis says, "No one ever told me that grief felt so much like fear." I'd never thought of grief that way, but he's right. Those emotions are closely related. In those vulnerable moments when you sit alone in your home, you realize your spouse will never return. In fact, this loneliness pervading the room will stay with you for the rest of your life as your constant companion. The missing will stay. The sense of loss will stay.

My home glowed with the warmth of the holy season, the scent of pine permeated each room. Music quietly played, telling the story of Christmas in so many meaningful ways, and it felt as though each note, each ornament, each tiny light, each candle, each gift, was mocking me.

Things will never be the same. The word normal has been stricken from the dictionary. Peace is for other people, but never again for me. This grief has me in such a strong grip that I fear I will be imprisoned forever. I am help-less, alone, tired—no, the word is weary. I am weary. I am afraid, afraid I will be alone from this day on, afraid of a new tomorrow, a different kind of life.

This is so hard. *So hard.*

I began to realize I had barely left the starting point in this journey. What a humbling revelation. There is a long way to go, and I'd better find a depend-able traveling companion, because there is no way I can do this on my own.

Lord, please walk with me and
show me the way. It's dark, and I can't see the
path ahead. Lead me, protect me, shower Your
love on me. I can't do this without You.

17

Left Behind

*The day he stepped into eternity was
the day my sense of mortality took on new
meaning. Life on earth does not go on forever.
One of us had to be the first to cross over.*

Three days after that snowy Sunday it was Christmas Day. I told my children I would host as I always had, and so my daughter and her family came late the night before after having their family Christmas in Chicago. My oldest son and his fiancée also arrived that evening and joined me at a Christmas Eve celebration at the home of some friends. Though I was unsure how I would handle it all, I wanted to do what we had always done. I knew having the children in the house would be good for me; their excitement and enthusiasm was just what I needed to lift the cloud of sorrow.

I agonized over the seating at dinner. Who should sit in Mel's seat at the head of the table? None of the options I came up with seemed right. Even at the moment we all gathered around for the blessing before the meal, I didn't know what I would do. And then one of my boys pulled out the chair and said, "Mom, you sit here."

The solution was logical, and yet it never occurred to me that I should be the one at the head of the table. Looking back, it was one of the many precious, invaluable gifts of that day. I am so thankful for my sons.

There were a couple of moments I had to quietly leave the room as the gifts were being opened. It was hard not to imagine how Mel would have enjoyed seeing the delight on the faces of the little boys as they opened their Lego sets. He'd had such fun building Lego creations with our boys when they were young, and now the grandsons couldn't wait to open similar boxes.

I remembered the year before Mel had drawn Michele's name, and I went shopping with him as he looked for the perfect gift for her. He was excited to give her the beautiful scarf he'd chosen at a small boutique in the city.

I remembered the year he had been given a framed photo of his favorite Yankees team, with one teammate, his back to the camera, having the name DeVries on his uniform.

But this Christmas wasn't measured in gifts or lights or songs of the season, or the beautiful, crisp white blanket of snow out my window. It was the love and comfort of my children and grandchildren around me, the warmth in a circle of good friends, and the certainty and peace knowing that my God was there, in control of everything, holding us up as He holds Mel near in an indescribably perfect eternity.

That's the reality. We are the ones left behind. We are left with the struggle of making sense of this unexpected loss. We are mandated to use it somehow for good.

It was our first Christmas, nine months after God took Mel to heaven. I was blessed to have the family God entrusted to me. Watching the children opening gifts, their sheer delight as only children can express, and seeing my kids interact as siblings do, I was grateful for this day.

Grace. That was God's gift to me at Christmas. Grace to make it through dinner without needing to leave the room and shed tears in private. Grace to enjoy the children as they ripped open their gifts and smiled in such delight at each one. Grace to have been inspired to give each of the grown boys one of the Christmas ties Mel had so loved wearing each December, and capturing that moment in a photograph.

Grace to take comfort in the silence filling the living room when the girls opened the picture I had framed for each of the couples—an image of their father with his signature smile, sitting on a rock in the summer sun. Grace to be blessed even while I felt such grief and loneliness in the midst of my family.

Just . . . grace.

> *My grace is sufficient for you, for my power is made perfect in weakness.*
>
> —II Corinthians 12:9

18

Beginning Again, Solo

*Many commented on how 'strong' I was. Little
did they know what was going on inside me.*

—JAMES R. WHITE GRIEVING: OUR PATH BACK TO PEACE

Writing is my way of expressing feelings, sharing the ideas and thoughts I am too insecure
to speak out loud. There is always a piece of myself in
the fiction, poetry, and posts on my blog and facebook.
This crazy roller coaster ride I'm on is just beginning,
but already I want to get off, go back to the starting
point, and choose a different ride. This one isn't fun.
I like the slow, safe, kiddie types. It's a Small World,
Pirates of the Caribbean, the miniature trains. Those
are my kind of entertainment. Keep it safe, easy, pre-
dictable, non-threatening. I'd much rather have those
safe things to record.

God wrote a different script for me. But He gave

me a tool to work with which is making all the difference. He gave me optimism. What a gift.

"In the book of life, the answers aren't in the back." Wise words, Charlie Brown, though if good answers were there, I might be more inclined to welcome in the New Year. Honestly, for a while, I didn't know if I should look forward to the new year or dread it.

Optimism is a good trait, one which got me through a lot of difficult years. The reality is, a lot of life is hard, painful, impossible. I prefer to temper those parts with the view that there is always, *always* something good to come out of the struggles. My parents were a great example of people who lived by that mantra. Life didn't treat them kindly those first few years after WWII as they moved to a new country, learned a new language and worked hard to make ends meet. Even so, I grew up with singing in the house, an ever-present faith in God, and a feeling of security and well-being that never wavered. They never let my brother and me know how poor we were.

My natural optimism tells me to look forward, never forgetting, always learning. So I'll not listen to Charlie Brown's dire prediction: "I'm afraid to be happy, because whenever I get too happy something bad always happens."

You're wrong, Charlie Brown. I'm not listening to you. Forward is the only way to go. The choice is in the direction we take, either the hopeful path or the dismal one.

I choose hope. I choose optimism. I choose to be happy. I choose to embrace this coming year and all the great things it will hold. I am so very richly blessed by my family and friends. And most of all by God. After all, He's the one in charge, and I know He has only my good in mind.

Bring on the new year. And shape up, Charlie Brown. You need a good dose of happy.

You are my God, and I will give you thanks; you are my God, and I will exalt you. Give thanks to the Lord, for he is good; his love endures forever.

—Psalm 118:28-29

19

Continuing . . . .

*Don't put on a happy face because you think it's
expected. Grief denied is grief unhealed*

—BARBARA BARTUCCI, NOBODY'S CHILD ANYMORE

Hard as Christmas was that first year, taking the
holiday decorations down was even harder. First
of all, I was once again alone. For several days, adults
and children had brought life to the house. On Christmas day twelve of us gathered, five of them children.
Then came New Year's Eve, alone. Not knowing what
to do with myself, eventually I decided to go to bed
early, and missed the ball drop in Times Square. I didn't
care. Judging by my mood, my sense of optimism was
on hiatus.

Now, as I took the ornaments off the trees, boxed
the wreaths, tucked the candles into their storage bins,
and put back the everyday paintings replaced with Mel's

carvings for the Christmas season, an immense sorrow overtook me. All this, these things making Christmas a joyful time, all of it reminded me of his absence this year. And worse, would from now on. My remaining time on this Earth will be spent without my husband by my side.

What a hard truth.

Here, once again, came a choice. Gazing out the window, I saw the sun shining on the surface of the pristine snow. It made me catch my breath, the dusting of millions of sparkling diamonds reflecting the light of the sun. Beauty is hidden everywhere. It's God's way of saying things will be all right. Maybe not right this minute, but the promise of it is there. The beauty *will be* visible if I am willing to look beyond today's circumstances. Those sparkles remind me of the meaning remaining in my life, even through the sadness.

I just need to find it.

Blessed are they who mourn,
for they will be comforted.

—Matthew 4:5

vision

your shadow falls
darkening pristine white sprays
of snow falling
for a moment
like white doves descending

fog distorts your form
pixellating features
flakes settle to earth
and you are gone

dissipated like melted
snow
were you there

or did I dream?

20

Birthday Blues

Grief teaches the steadiest mind to waver.

—SOPHOCLES

I spent my first birthday stranded in my house without my husband. A snowy day, most schools had been canceled due to bad roads. And honestly, I had nowhere I wanted to go by myself. It seemed wrong to celebrate without Mel, though I would have jumped at the chance to go somewhere, do something had I been asked. My daughter had planned to drive in from Chicago but weather conditions kept her away. My son in Milwaukee had similar issues. My youngest son had already invited me for the following Sunday because of the snowstorm on my actual birthday. Not a great day.

Granted, the weather kept everyone away this particular year. A brutal winter is not a widow's friend, especially not in the first twelve months. In the scheme of things, it was just another day. But because I had lost my husband ten months prior, he wouldn't be bringing me flowers or take me to dinner or call during the day to say "Happy birthday." It was lonely. I have to admit I had a pity party that day. I did feel neglected. Even the mailman failed to show—due to weather, but still. It was probably the worst birthday I've ever had.

Looking back, I realize how self-centered I was, but it showed me something. Sometimes a negative is necessary to see a positive, in fact, a multitude of positives. Over my lifetime, I've been gifted with many wonderful birthdays even though I didn't deserve or expect them. God blesses me in so many ways. One day, *one day* out of the many is not bad odds. I'm learning to be thankful for each morning I awaken to a fresh start. They are all good days with new potential and promise. How I use them determines how I feel about myself at the end.

God, You have chosen to give me breath
on this day. I choose to thank You.

This is the day the Lord has made;
let us rejoice and be glad in it.

—PSALM 118:24

21

Living In The Rear View Mirror

*There are moments when I would like to
tell people that, until you experience a loss
this big, everything else is amateur night.*

—Ruth Coughlin

How much time can you spend looking back and still expect to move forward? That's the million dollar question. It's okay to remember, in fact, it's a good thing. Going through pictures, reminiscing over the last big trip we took to Italy just a year before and thankful for the unforgettable times we had with close friends is a comfort. Remembering the beauty of Cinque Terra and the peace and tranquility of Lake Como, two of our favorite places in Italy, brings a smile to my face and lightness to my heart.

Switch frames, and we're in the kitchen having a disagreement about what to do with our flooring. He's adamant we need ceramic tile. I hate ceramic tile and want wood. We can't see eye to eye. I tell him tile is cold; he says we can install a heating unit. I say tile is killer on dropped dishes—one piece becomes millions. He says wood can be scratched. On it goes, the Push-Me-Pull-You of many of our arguments.

Another scene plays out, and now we're in the Netherlands, walking the cemetery where Mel's grandparents are buried. His face is a study as he sees their names etched on the old gravestones. We attend services in his father's old church, and though he can't understand a word, he is transfixed. This is his heritage; this is where his father worshiped; this house is where his grandparents raised his father.

Later in the day we visit the small town where I was born, and he marvels over the lovely little canal running through the center of the small burg. We walk by the house my father used as a barber shop on the main floor, its windows overlooking the canal. We see the windows of the apartment my family lived in above the shop. I show him the overhang at my uncle's house where my father hid from the Nazi soldiers during the war. The experience draws us close, the shared heritage and the very act of being in those places gives us a sense of oneness.

Then a flash to another disagreement resulting in an actual verbal battle, the anger and frustration, each believing we are right, the impasse we seemed to reach in many of those. Then finding our way back again. Somehow, sidestepping the issue that brought the argument in the first place, we agree to disagree.

So many times we reach an impasse in a marriage, and I know Mel and I often blew them out of proportion. Eager to be the one who was right, we refused to see the other's point of view. I blame the stubbornness on my Dutch heritage. But that's not fair—we all have control over what we say and do.

There are happy times in those looks in the rearview mirror to counteract the hard stuff. I'm hopeful over time the good memories will overtake all the rest. We have so many wonderful family times to carry forward. Maybe some of the negatives will be viewed with a sense of humor someday.

The important nugget here is we are all human. My husband was not perfect. He had a temper, though that did lessen as he aged. He tended to be a bit stubborn and opinionated, but I must admit to those things myself. I'm just as flawed as the next person, though I hate to acknowledge it.

The thing is, there were so many good qualities about Mel to recall, and those are the things I choose to concentrate on.

I look forward to the day I can talk about all of who Mel was without pain. To remember with a warm sense of love and gratitude for having had him in my life. The 'remember whens' should be warm and fuzzy, the pictures of him viewed with love and a grateful heart. I long for that time. In the meantime, it's okay not to be there yet. Month by month the sharp edge of grief dulls a little bit. This is, after all, a process—one with no definitive time frame.

> *Lord, I can't see it right now—the end of*
> *the pain and loss. I know I need to trust*
> *You to lead me to a place of quiet rest.*
> *Give me the endurance to keep going.*

22

Being Isolated

It is in the shelter of each other that people live.

—IRISH PROVERB

Seven weeks into first grade as I walked home down our gravel road with my brother, I fell to the ground and could not get up. We were almost home, right in front of the house and close to the driveway, when it happened. My brother ran screaming for our parents, terrified that something awful had just happened. He was right.

Because of my complete paralysis, the doctor's initial diagnosis was polio, a virus-based transmittable illness several children in our area had contracted. I was on the brink of death during the two months the paralysis persisted. Eventually, the doctor determined that instead of polio I had rheumatic fever, an illness caused by strep throat (group A streptococcus). Not only did it cause high fever and immobility, the virus also damaged my heart and resulted in my isolation at home for the next ten years.

I spent the first two years bedridden and on daily shots of penicillin administered by my mother. The state of Washington where we lived provided homeschooling, a visiting teacher who came for an hour three times a week to go over lessons in all the required subjects. Mrs. Faulkner became my link to the school world, bringing me books, a movie projector, and a screen along with films such as *Heidi, Black Beauty* and others suitable for my age. I developed a love for reading and soon had books sent in an exchange program via mail from our local library. Those days when the package of books arrived were the highlights of the week.

During all this time my brother continued attending school every day without me. Though I don't remember much about those years, I remember feeling isolated. He got to go to school, play with other kids, run around at recess. Or run at all. I had no friends to play with, no real portal to the world around me other than letters to several pen pals. I was lonely.

After my husband died I felt a profound sense of isolation again, but this time, it was different because I had lots of people around me—family, friends, my church—yet that isolation was as real and painful as in my childhood.

My fragile heart became bruised with each careless statement. You know the kind: *You should be thankful you had him as long as you did. He's better off now. At least you know where he is. Other people are much worse off than you. You'll get over it pretty soon. Why don't you do some volunteer work and get your mind off your loss? Maybe you'll meet someone new.* And the ever asked *how are you?* (Translation: I'm asking, but I don't really want an honest answer so please just say okay and we'll change the subject).

Ouch. Ever feel totally alone in a room full of people? Yeah, that island was me. I only wanted to stay home and wrap up in a blanket for the next decade.

It's hard enough being a 'one' in the midst of 'twos.' Twice as hard when you recently were in the 'two' category. How do you navigate in this new world without your partner? There's no user's manual provided to the widowed. All that being said, the next chapter should make perfect sense to those of you on a little island similar to mine.

I do wonder sometimes if those ten years of being alone and away from other kids my age might have been preparation for the events of these past months. Maybe God was preparing me for a different kind of isolation.

Never will I leave you, never will I forsake you.

—HEBREWS 13:5

23

I've Lost Control

*How is sanity determined? Could it be
that no one actually possesses that gift?*

So many emotions come out during the grieving
process. I had no idea what I was in for when my
journey began; there was no frame of reference against
which to measure myself. I thought I was the only person who had anger issues, heard all sorts of noises in
the night while trying to sleep, *can you say 'neurotic?'*,
couldn't remember anything, not one single thing, lost
the ability to read a book (what's the use when you
don't understand a word of what you're reading, and
you stay on the same page for ten minutes or more?).
. . . Well, you get the picture.

Because I have absolutely no sense of direction,
I was fearful of driving places I'd never been before,
terrified of getting lost even though that's an entirely

illogical fear in this day of Siri and GPS. Uncertainty and fear of, well, everything, had me at a definite disadvantage. I'm in charge of finding my way? This won't go well.

I was pretty sure I was insane. In the pit one day, I wrote the following;

I have gone completely crazy. I know this because I can't remember anything, have no motivation, and I'm more exhausted than ever in my life. I can't follow a simple thread of conversation, nor can I comprehend a sentence. I can't knit, or write a cohesive thought. I've become a robot, moving and responding with no sense of purpose or will of my own, and, most of the time, without feeling. I'm eternally restless despite fatigue. And I'm so alone, so isolated.

But that song...Chris Tomlin's "God of Angel Armies" has been in my head since March 17 on a continuous track night and day, over and over and over. I can repeat every word.

I have lost control. My mind is a car in an empty parking lot.

Lord, I have never needed direction more than
I do now. I need you to help me walk this path;
I need you to show me the way, to reassure
me that I'll be okay. Lord, I need . . . You.

24

When Your Loved One Is Gone

Sometimes when one person is missing,
the whole world seems depopulated.

—ALPHONSE DE LAMARTINE

My parents lived across the country from us and came out once a year to visit. Our financial situation didn't allow us many trips with our family of five, so we were grateful for their willingness to come to us. At the age of 70, my mom was diagnosed with Alzheimer's. It became impossible for my parents to make the journey to Michigan. Consequently, our roles reversed, and I was the one making the trip twice a year.

My mom died after a hard struggle. I promised my father I would stay for two weeks beyond the funeral to help with whatever he needed me to do.

Almost immediately after the funeral, he asked me to go through Mom's closet and dresser drawers with him and decide what to do with her belongings. The entire room was stripped of my mother's things by the time two days had passed. He kept nothing—it was almost as if he couldn't bear to have reminders of her. At the time I didn't think much of that, assuming he wanted my help while I was there so that he wouldn't have to make decisions alone.

Looking back, knowing what I know, I realize he believed what many widows and widowers do; an immediate purge will help the pain go away. Over the years he found it didn't do that, and there were indications of regret.

In my bedroom, the chair where Mel laid his clothes at the end of the day sets beside the window. It often frustrated me that he didn't put things away after use, either in the hamper or in the closet or drawer. The day he died he had thrown his favorite red fleece, jeans and socks on the chair and changed to compression clothes for his run. That night when I walked into the room in my zombie state, the first thing I saw was the red fleece. I stared at it, all sorts of thoughts swirling through my head—confusion, pain, disbelief, denial.

For weeks, I continued to see the fleece each time I walked into the room. I couldn't touch it—believing it would be a betrayal to move it. And yet how strange to leave those things on the chair as if waiting for his return. What a weird combination of feeling guilt (if

I move the clothing, does that mean I don't want to remember?), irreverence (am I diminishing his importance by putting his things away?) and obligation (I must leave them there for X amount of time). Finally I removed his clothes from the chair. That day I felt a sense of reluctance mixed with sorrow. Putting those items away forced me to acknowledge the reality that he was indeed gone.

One morning a few months after his death, I awoke knowing it was time to empty Mel's closet. He would not come back. The clothes he once wore served no purpose hanging in the closet. A local shelter needed men's clothing for the men they helped get back on their feet, and in my heart I felt Mel pushing me to give them his wardrobe.

Here's one of the bizarre things about cleaning out the closet of someone who has died: you feel a strange combination of relief, guilt, sadness, regret and incredible loss.

As I folded each piece and placed it in a box, I remembered the time Mel had worn that item, how handsome he looked in this sweater, that shirt, those ties. I smiled as I folded the jazzy socks he loved to wear, remembered how he had this gift for putting things together to look especially nice. Bittersweet snapshots flashed through the lens of memory with those items.

Exhausted at the end of the day, I knew in my

heart the rightness of my decision to give his clothes away.

I kept the red fleece. In the hundreds of pictures I have of him, the fleece shows up time and time again as his favorite piece of comfortable clothing. Some things I reserved; I needed to hold them for myself. Before I gave items away I had my boys go through and choose things they wanted, and my daughter chose some things for my son-in-law. That was such a great decision—I would have never been able to choose for them.

Each of us remembers Mel in our own way. We often share stories as we sit around the Thanksgiving table or as we relax after Christmas dinner. The time has come for these memories to be shared; they are priceless, and they keep him alive in our hearts.

I thank my God every time I remember you.

—Philippians 1:3

25

Living Gluten-Free
Is Not For The Fainthearted

I have no peace, no quietness:
I have no rest, but only turmoil.

—Job 3:26

Nine months prior to his death, Mel was diagnosed with celiac disease. In many ways I would have preferred it be me with it, because he was a lover of everything flour related. Cakes, cookies, donuts, breads; he never met one he didn't like. The fact that cereal, pasta, soups, pizza and hundreds of other things were included in the banned foods didn't help, either. I became a label reader. If it didn't contain gluten but was processed in a factory processing foods with gluten, it went on the banned list. I was vigilant. He was miserable.

Going to a restaurant posed challenges. Did they

offer a gluten-free menu? If so, did they designate a dedicated space to prepare the food? Did they use special pans, spoons, cutting boards, colanders and utensils exclusively meant for gluten-free foods?

I had to pitch all our cookware and buy new because ours was Teflon coated and the scratches might contain gluten fragments; the spatulas, cutting boards, cake, cookie and pie pans, the toaster, the bread maker, all went into a donation box…and on and on. Needless to say, our budget took a huge hit. Not only did I need to replace all those things, but the 'gluten free' notification on food items automatically doubled or tripled the price.

Trips to the grocery store took hours as I read each ingredient on every label. I readjusted recipes, tried to be creative in the lunch items Mel took to work. I made various new dishes to offer delicious meals with no hint of gluten. It was torture for both of us. In the end, my diligence didn't seem to address the issues bringing the diagnosis in the first place. He still had cramps, discomfort, diarrhea, and reflux.

I did everything correctly. Beyond careful, I monitored every bite going into Mel's mouth. But the feeling persisted that it might be more than food. I rationalized the doctors should know if we needed to pursue other avenues when symptoms continued.

Mel's father died of a heart attack at the age of

54. He'd been a smoker and previously had a heart attack. The second one took his life. Two siblings had heart-related issues. Mel's doctors knew of his family history.

Here's where guilt stepped in and took center stage. I should have made him take me with him to his appointments. I should have said, hey, is this discomfort, this pain, possibly a sign of heart issues? I should have shoved it in their faces, right? Should have. The fact is I didn't, and now I look back and wonder.

That's the crazy kind of niggling that goes on after the fact. Why didn't I say something? Insist on going with him to appointments? And then, if I had, would it have made a difference? The doctors attending Mel after his heart attack cited a likely genetic predisposition, something he was born with. Still, there's that nagging doubt. That guilt.

One famous television evangelist would call what I was doing *stinkin' thinkin.'* I struggle with the doubt even now. The what-ifs following a death can eat at you, erode your confidence. Did you do everything you could? You wake in the middle of the night with yet another scenario. I carried this guilt for months.

One day in a conversation with a friend I mentioned Mel's father had died at an early age. We had just discussed the doctors' conclusion as to Mel's cause of death. I don't remember how the conversation went, but at one point my friend looked at me and said, "Terri, did it occur to you that you had him those extra fourteen years (longer than his dad had lived) because you took such good care of him?" Wow. That stopped me in my tracks. She was right; his father had not listened to his doctors when they said to quit smoking, to take better care of his health. Mel had done everything right, and I had done everything right. An extra fourteen years was a tremendous gift.

That conversation impacted me. It helped put things in perspective, to realize my guilt was self-inflicted. Only God knows the year, the month, the week, the day, the hour of your death, and He planned it long before you were born. He wrote it in His book. Who am I to argue with that?

Whatever your guilt, whatever your shoulda-coulda-woulda list might be, remember Who is in control, and lay your guilt down. God will take care of it all.

"For I know the plans I have for you," declares the Lord, "plans to prosper you and not to harm you, plans to give you hope and a future."

—JEREMIAH 29:11

26

When You Just Can't Pray

What a tremendous relief to discover that we don't
need to do anything to prove ourselves to God.

—DESMOND TUTU

The words of the title probably sound irreverent—
what do I mean you can't pray? Maybe you've
never had a time in your life when you couldn't. Why
would a person who professes to be a Christian *not* be
able to pray?

Twice in my life I was utterly helpless to form
the words. The first was when I had a breakdown in
my forties and my whole world twisted out of control.
Though I won't go into detail, I will say it was, up to
that point, the most painful and challenging time in
my adult life. Maybe it was preparation for what was
to come, but regardless, I found it impossible to pray.

I had many praying for me, a fact which I believe

helped lift me out of the despair. The long road to recovery spanned several years, most of which I spent working hard at recovery.

The second time I was unable to pray was the period starting March 17th, the day Mel died, and extending a long while beyond. Again many were praying for me, and knowing so carried me.

Sure, I screamed at God, I ranted and shook my fist, but that's not exactly prayer by my definition. That's just plain raw anger. Fortunately, I found myself in good company. Many of the saints in the Bible showed anger towards God, too. I felt no guilt for the anger because I believe God gave us the ability to be angry as a means of expression, a way to get our feelings out. Anger exacerbates our frustrations and helplessness to change or correct a situation. We are pointed to the One who has all the answers, the One who knows how to read the map of this perilous journey. After all, He's the One who made the map.

Anger also shows us our dependence on God. Without His guidance, I would not have found my way along this path I'm on. Today I'm traveling without any instruction, but no maps or GPS systems are needed. He's leading. All I have to do is follow.

All *you* have to do is follow, too.

Since you are my rock and my fortress, for the sake of your name, lead and guide me.

—Psalm 31:3

27

I'll Never Accomplish Anything Ever Again (and other excuses)

It's like I have this large black hole in my brain
and it's sucking the life out of me. The answers
are in there so I sit for hours and stare. No matter
how hard and long I look, I only see darkness.

—KATIE MCGARRY, PUSHING THE LIMITS

I can't concentrate. Therefore, I have a reason to do nothing. The house is clean enough. I don't *need* to wash my clothes. Tomorrow is a better day to make that call. The bills can wait. It's just too painful to do that. Because you know, I'm a recent widow. *Hello, my name is Terri, and I'm a widow.*

Widow.

I hate that word with every ounce of strength in me. It's an ugly, awful word. It should be banished from the English language.

Yet I use it as a crutch. Yes, a payment was missed on my electric bill, but I'm a recent *widow,* and therefore I have a good reason. Of course I should have gone to that meeting, but I'm a *widow,* and it's hard doing things alone. People should feel sorry for me because I'm a *widow.*

No, the house didn't get cleaned this week, but you know, I'm a *widow,* and I just have so much to deal with these days.

Did I mention I find the word widow demeaning, because it makes me appear to be a weak person? I mean, read the stories in the Bible. Widows are placed in the category with orphans, a helpless group without family. Funny, I seem to want things both ways—it's an excuse, and yet I find it demeaning. Hmm.

Widow.

That's not me. Bill's wife, or Helen next door, or my friends Petra and Sue, they're widows. Not me. Then again, it's that catch-all word covering all the things I can't—no, wait—don't want to do. And there it is, another unattractive truth. When did I start using the word widow as my excuse?

At what point do I pull myself up out of my pity and begin to take ownership? The fact that I'm asking the question is more than likely my answer.

Now.

Now is the time to begin. Not every minute of every day. Not every day of the week. But it has to start if I'm ever to get out of the quagmire of grief.

What do I do? Maybe the answer is as close as a whispered prayer to God, the Healer of all hurt, the Great Physician, who can repair even the most broken of hearts. That's where I begin. That's where I need to continue.

Every. Day. For. The. Rest. Of. My. Life.

Lord, you know the condition of my heart.
You know every feeling of pain and despair,
every lonely moment. You know my grief.
Heal me, walk with me, give me peace.

28

Let The Healing Begin

You can't stop the waves, but you can learn to surf.

—JOSEPH GOLDSTEIN

Shortly after Mel died, the funeral home which took care of his remains asked me to stop in. They gave me the required paperwork, his ashes, a how-to-and-when to-do list, and information on an organization called Griefshare. The brochure said a local church offered 13 sessions, but most of them were done for the spring season. The next series would begin in the fall. The funeral director encouraged me to keep it in mind for late summer.

By August I began thinking about this thing called Griefshare. I checked online and found it is a national organization offering a film series to groups interested in helping those who are grieving. A church not far away from me was hosting the series beginning in

September. No sign-up necessary. That appealed to me, because what if I didn't like it and then felt obligated? So I made a note of the date and time, and I showed up.

For thirteen weeks I showed up.

The leaders followed a simple format. Half an hour of going around the circle, telling your story, telling about your week, the ups and downs. The beautiful part of this was that as each person spoke, heads nodded around the circle, as understanding permeated the room.

We watched a 30-minute video, each week a different aspect of grief; what to expect, suggestions for making it through this valley of grief, interviews with those who knew firsthand what we were learning. Then a break for coffee, water, and cookies. For the last segment, we broke into two groups to discuss the film and its impact, our takeaway, and reactions related to our journey. The last ten or so minutes we met as a unified group for announcements and closing devotions.

We averaged 24 to 27 people in attendance. At one of the first meetings, as we were going around the circle, I thought, *what a lot of sadness lives in this room.* Each loss was different: a spouse, a child, a parent, a dear friend, a sibling. Each story was unique: an accident, a murder, a long illness, a sudden death, a suicide. The common thread was the pain. I have to admit it was depressing at first.

Gradually, as the weeks progressed, laughter became interspersed with tears, and funny stories came out of experiences. A sense of camaraderie built as trust grew. Each of us had had our heart broken. Though our paths were as different as our personalities, we understood each other at a profoundly deep level.

About halfway through the thirteen sessions I found myself drawn to a few of the women who were also widows. We have since become friends and still see each other occasionally for lunch or dinner. It's all about the common bond, the fact that each of us understands the particular pain of losing a husband. They are farther down the path than I, and so they are encouragers, assuring me that I will survive and life will go on.

Griefshare is an excellent organization offering help and support to those in the throes of grief. The videos are helpful as they explore aspects of the emotions we experience because of loss. Just being in a room with others who know what you are feeling and who validate your grief is a healing process.

I am thankful for the people I met through the program. They added a new dimension to my circle of friends. It was a simple bond. We needed each other, we understood each other, we supported each other.

Praise be to the God and Father of our Lord Jesus Christ, the Father of compassion and the God of all comfort, who comforts us in all our troubles so that we can comfort those in any trouble with the comfort we ourselves have received from God.

—II Corinthians 1:3-4

29

Regret

Guilt is perhaps the most
painful companion to death.

—Elisabeth Kubler-Ross

And there it is, rearing its ugly, all-knowing head. Things you said you can't take back. Things you should have said and now never can. Things you did (or didn't do) which can't be done (or undone). It's a long, embarrassing, miserable list.

As if this grief thing isn't hard enough. As if I don't have enough to deal with.

A never-ending film runs through my mind: all the times I had an opportunity to say something to bolster Mel, the little things I could have done to make ordinary moments more special. Sometimes words spoken in anger or frustration play in my head, and I want to take them back. I should have tried harder to understand, to be helpful, to encourage, to be more loving. *Should* have.

We all tend to dwell on those negative things once we have the gift of hindsight. Too bad we can't see ahead to prevent those words from coming out. Too bad we can't do the uplifting things we thought about but never did. That's the thing about life—once an action is taken or a word is spoken, they can't be taken back. No do-overs. No 'Oops, let me rephrase that.'

There are some things that never got resolved: I don't think there's a couple who doesn't have issues needing to be addressed at some point. The thing about death is you never get to take care of those things. If you had an ongoing disagreement about something important, it will never be resolved. Maybe your spouse was right, and you didn't get around to admitting it. Maybe you couldn't let the issue go even though it wasn't that big of a deal. Maybe you only needed to say "I'm sorry," but pride (or stubbornness) held you back.

What if, maybe then, if only.

Another guilt producer I experienced was when I found myself having a good time for the first time after my husband died. How could I? What was wrong with me when I was supposed to be in mourning? What would everyone think?

Out for dinner with friends, a comment made me laugh out loud. One of my companions looked at me and said, "Terri, it's so good to hear you laugh." It made me realize that I *was* allowed, that maybe they *needed* to hear my laughter to know that I was healing.

Life goes on for us all. Mel would want me to enjoy our friends, to find things to laugh about. He would not expect me to hold on to regrets, to blame myself for past transgressions. I'm gradually letting go of that particular guilt, remembering what my friend said and knowing he was so right. It's good to feel happy, to relish time with people who care about me.

I believe Mel smiles every time he sees me enjoying life.

Those who sow in tears will reap with songs of joy.

—Psalm 126:5

30

Murphy Has A Law, And He's Not Afraid To Use It

Anything that can go wrong will go wrong.

—MURPHY

It may be unique to me, though I've heard many others have had similar problems. Murphy surfaced soon after Mel died. I've already mentioned several issues—the garage door, my car battery, iritis in my eyes, the chimney problem, etc.

By the time I got to the ten-month marker, I thought I was on the road to equilibrium. Not so much. First, my furnace died on one of the coldest days on record in January. Of course it happened on a Saturday, but I got my repair guy out, and he did the repair.

A week later my landline phone died. The internet connection didn't connect. I did all the tests necessary to assure myself I couldn't fix it, and scheduled an appointment with a repairman. Then the phone came back on. The internet worked. So I canceled the service call and breathed a sigh of relief. And it all went down again. For three days I dealt with the on-again-off-again problem. I set another appointment with the phone company.

The same weekend (yes, it was a weekend again) I went into one of my spare bedrooms to retrieve a clock for downstairs. As I lifted it, a brown stain on the table caught my eye. I looked up. There, big and ugly, was a cracked brown area indicating a leak. Great. Now the roof. Which needed to be replaced, of course.

All these things translated into inconveniences and/or expenses, neither of which I needed or wanted in my life at this point. I must say I really despise Mr. Murphy. I never liked him much in the first place, but those days as I thought about the string of things going wrong, I had a whole new hatred for him.

I just want to know when it will be over. Let's see; the count is up to . . . fourteen? That's a good round number. Enough already. I'm done.

So, Lord, what's the plan?

31

Roller Coaster Syndrome

The mind has a dumb sense of vast
loss—that is all. It will take mind and memory
months and possibly years to gather the details
and know the whole extent of the loss.

—MARK TWAIN

When my kids were younger, I took them to a theme park not far from where we lived. Though small, Deer Park Funland had several of the crazy rides they loved, and it helped pass a summer day.

I am not a thrill seeker, mostly because I get very dizzy when circular or up-and-down movements are involved. But because my kids wanted me to go with them on one particular ride, the good mom in me gave in. The ride was one of those spin-around ones where both the car and the entire mechanism spun separately. Double the fun. The attendant came around to check the safety bars were in the lock position. He then sauntered to the center shaft where the motor was housed to start the ride, and immediately tuned out.

Only a few seconds in I realized the bar on my seat had not locked shut. By this time we were spinning around at a pretty good clip, and the attendant was somewhere in la la land, paying no attention to anything associated with the machinery. I grabbed the bar, pulled it toward me, and held on for dear life, praying the ride would end soon. I had visions of being catapulted off the seat to my death or (at the very least) to my significant injury. Though I'm sure the ride wasn't an unusually long one, it seemed to go on forever. By the time it finally ended, I was a wreck. I don't think I stopped shaking until we were safely home again.

My second brush with terror was at Cedar Point on their newest roller coaster, the Blue Streak. It was nearing sunset and would be the last ride of the day. Issues with carsickness most of my life kept me from rides going up and down rapidly or in circles, but my daughter coaxed me into getting on with her. This wasn't going to go well, but she was so persuasive. . . .

Looking back, I admit the view was spectacular. The sun had begun dipping into the western horizon, casting an orange glow over the theme park as we sped up and over the many undulations of the course. Though I ended up feeling a bit sick, the ride was memorable.

Only at the highest peaks could we overlook the entire park, a breathtaking scene. I hasten to add I'll never ride that roller coaster again.

In those early months after Mel died I had that same feeling of terror. If I didn't hold on tight enough, something bad would happen, so I used all the energy I had to pull the bar of sanity toward myself. Had I stopped to think, though, I would have realized that, just as the centrifugal force kept me in my seat on the first ride, God would keep me in place. I needed to relax, let the grief take me where it will, allow the process to go as it was meant to go. Much less effort is required if I sit back and finish the ride.

Someday I hope to look back at this time of grief and remember the beauty, because it can be found even in the midst of great sorrow. Everyday graces are waiting to be seen and felt, whether through a crocus blooming in the snow, a friend bringing brownies or a meaningful Easter service. I can't always see them in the middle of a hard day, but I imagine hindsight is a good lens for those days when I miss them.

Hold on tight. Keep your eyes open. Watch for the breathtaking views about to begin. Be patient while you wait. And trust that at the end of the ride you'll step into the sense of peace you so desire.

Peace I leave with you; my peace I give you.

—JOHN 14:27

32

Being Marginalized

Don't ignore those who grieve. They
crave your touch, your hugs, your love.

Many years ago, women dressed in black for a full year after losing a family member. Then they went to dark hues of gray, purple, brown and navy the second year. Men wore black armbands. Black wreaths were placed on doors to indicate a loss, curtains drawn, mirrors covered. The dead were honored, the mourning acknowledged, and those left behind were shown respect well after the death.

Today we have no indicators to pinpoint the bereaved. You might pass a new widower as you walk in the mall, or sit down to dinner in a restaurant near parents grieving the loss of a child, and be oblivious to the loss. In this modern age, we lack those outward signs.

More importantly, though, the widow and widower find themselves in a unique, difficult position. Where they used to be two, they are now one. In our society, one is an uncomfortable number for a group of friends who are couples. At first, they try to accommodate the single person, but as time passes, those attempts become longer between. It's awkward.

At the same time, since we have no visible symbol of loss such as the black dress or armband, those people tend to forget that a person might still be in deep grief. I was as guilty as the next person to think that after some months the hard part must be over.

You see the widow at an event and she's smiling. The widower comes to church and talks with the guys like he used to. Soon the death that changed everything about their lives is forgotten by friends. After all, the bereaved person seems to be fine, right?

Being marginalized is a difficult concept to explain. It basically means the person is set aside, dismissed, excluded, deemed less. *Less.* The dictionary defines marginalize like this: *to place in a position of marginal importance, influence, or power.* We all know a margin is the space next to the body of a letter; the edge, the border, the fringe, a limit beyond which something ceases to exist or to be desirable. Ouch.

The honest truth is, many couples are uncomfortable being with a single person.

So let's talk. Before Mel died, I was guilty of thinking I should invite a widowed friend over, but never got beyond the thinking. Sunday dinner. A night out to a movie or play. A cup of coffee on a wintry morning. Lunch in the middle of a rainy month. Breakfast on a somber fall day. A drive in the country on a bright spring day. A picnic on the beach on a lovely summer afternoon. A phone call. A card with a brief message. Flowers from your garden. All these are simple but meaningful things to do for a lonely person. If you sit and think about it, you'll discover many more options.

I never realized how much these small things meant for a widow or widower. I had no idea what a huge part loneliness plays in day-to-day life. Dinner alone, church alone, trips alone, shopping alone, important days alone. Evenings at home alone. The reality of it doesn't sink in until you are the person who has to face aloneness.

I can't tell you how many times I've seen or heard something and thought, *oh I have to tell Mel. He'd love that. I bet he'd know the answer. I'll ask him that person's name—he'd remember.*

Sometimes I wish we still had those old conventions of armbands or the black clothing to identify the grieving ones. I know I'd make an effort to express my sympathies if that were the norm today. Instead, we who lost someone wear our grief on the inside, where most don't see it. I believe we've lost a bit of the respect for the bereaved, a respect we used to take for granted.

If the opportunity to offer your respects arises, regardless of the form it takes, do it. You will never regret it. It's never too late. Because someday you may be on the receiving end.

> *A new command I give you: Love one another. As I have loved you, so must you love one another.*
>
> —JOHN 3:26

33

Secondary Losses— The Ripple Effect

If you wonder how long grief lasts,
I'll tell you: as long as it takes.

The stone leaves my grandson's hand and strikes the calm surface of the water, immediately causing a rippling effect as it sinks below the surface. I watch the rings gradually spread across the water, making bigger and bigger circles. What a great analogy, I think. One little stone sinks, but in the process all sorts of chaos is caused on the water's surface. In the same way, Mel's death began the rippling, affecting the ordinary things of life.

I mentioned earlier that my husband died just a month before taxes were due. He always did the filing, got the necessary information about our investments, and made sure all the information I collected got integrated into the forms. He hadn't done the compiling yet, and I found myself with a deadline and minimal information. The burden of doing taxes had shifted to me. I am thankful a good friend stepped up and got the taxes done for me.

This was the first of many tasks left to me, and I was overwhelmed, especially that first year. The work of grief is exhausting in itself, let alone handling the to-dos. Struggling to deal with Mel's sudden death, now all these *things* were my responsibility. Power washing the deck, doing the staining, getting out the lawn furniture (and putting it back in the storage shed in fall), manning the grill, mowing the lawn and trimming; keeping the car updated on oil changes, tire rotations, etc.; cleaning the garage, doing household repairs, cleaning the gutters spring, summer and fall, trimming the trees and bushes—it never ended. These things became my job, along with the duties I already had. And I had to drive myself everywhere, find parking, walk longer distances, this after many years of being dropped off by my husband.

I remember someone saying she was so busy with the added duties that she didn't have time or energy to do things with her friends. "They don't understand," she said, "that I am now doing the work of two people."

It's true. I found I either had to find someone to do those chores, or I had to figure out a way to do them myself. I was angry at being so bogged down with the extra responsibilities. In those first few months, having to deal with it all was exhausting. I had all I could do to put one foot in front of the other. The unfairness was incomprehensible to me.

We discussed this situation in one of the Griefshare sessions, and the leaders explained these were secondary losses—the loss of things our spouse did which we now must do ourselves. We've lost our companion, but we've also lost the helper who did many of the chores. Navigating this foreign territory is intimidating. No wonder we have doubts about our ability to manage our many layers of grief—sorrow is compounded by the tangential things attached to the loss. It's a chain reaction.

It takes courage, this tackling of unforeseen problems. You can't ignore the leak in the roof or the dead battery in your car. Burying yourself under an afghan in hopes problems will go away while you hide—that's not going to work. I have to admit I did a lot of self-pitying when things went awry. Self pity didn't help the situation, though, and I still had to deal with it at some point. If you don't make the call when the furnace first goes out, it most definitely will get colder in the house as time passes.

The ripple effect of my husband's passing is still going on. The rings aren't as evident as before, and I'm learning to handle each challenge with more confidence than when the first ripple appeared. That doesn't mean I've 'gotten over' his death. What it does mean is I've learned to adjust, to work with the reality. Some days I still feel panic, helplessness, anxiety, fear, anger, guilt, failure, emptiness, sadness, loneliness—the list goes on. Normal feelings, but less intense, less frequent. New feelings have edged in and taken over most of the time. Hope, peace, joy, contentment, thankfulness, and an incredible ability to appreciate my life as it now is.

My faith has grown. There was a time when I wasn't sure I had faith anymore, and that, too, was normal. I will never understand the why of my situation, and maybe that doesn't matter. I've begun to accept my new life, and that I believe is the key. I can only move forward: the choice I have to make is *how* I do that, either with anger and resentment or with acceptance and a positive attitude.

Your secondary losses may look very different from mine. Your circumstances may vary. The choice is yours; how will you accept what life has given you?

> *God grant me the serenity to accept the things*
> *I cannot change; courage to change the things*
> *I can; and wisdom to know the difference.*
>
> —Reinhold Niebuhr

34

The Gift Of Pain

*Only in experiencing the depth of grief
can we understand the height of joy.*

I've often heard the comment, "In a perfect world we wouldn't have to deal with pain." As idealistic as that may be, imagine what a world without pain would be like. From the day of your birth, you'd never experience pain in either the physical or emotional sense. Broken arms wouldn't hurt; neither would a cut or abrasion. Hearts would never be broken by a cruel act or harsh word. We would live a flat-lined life.

How then would we know real joy? Wouldn't everything be even-keeled? No highs or lows, no extremes of any kind. Until you experience the deepest of pain, you cannot fully appreciate the lack of it. Pain, grief, hurt—all those are necessary parts of our lives. Without them, we would be unable to measure joy, happiness, contentment.

Even in my initial state of shock I felt the pain of losing Mel. It was dull thanks to the insulation shock provided, but still present. Over time, pain intensified as the shock wore off and I had to deal with it unbuffered. When you are in the throes of loss it's impossible to imagine a time when things will level out, diminish, become less painful. Being told your pain is a gift is incomprehensible, cruel. But it's true. Think about this: your spouse mattered, and now he is gone. That hurts. The reality is undeniable, the pain of your grief is palpable. Were it not so, the person wasn't significant, and life would go on with only the slightest bump in the road.

You may not believe this now, but sometime in the future you will realize the pain has changed, softened, become easier and lighter to bear.

My moments of feeling normal came to me gradually and in small spurts, each time blessing me with the knowledge my sanity was returning, however fleeting. I began to trust that I could step out of the cocoon shock had built around me and accept the new territory out there. Scary as that was, I took those steps believing it would be safe. In early summer, just a couple of months after Mel died, I spent a lot of time in my back yard working in the flower gardens. The sunshine, the colors of flowers in bloom, the bushes filling in with leaves and the weeds that needed pulling—these all helped ground me, gave me firm earth to stand on outside of my cocoon of grief.

Most of the summer I spent time pulling weeds, trimming bushes, deadheading flowers, spreading mulch. Working outdoors was the most therapeutic thing I could have done. The sunshine warmed me while the nature around me nurtured me. I wore sunglasses when the iritis in my eyes made it difficult to be in the light, and I used a heating pad in the evenings when my back gave me issues—anything to enable me to be out in the warm summer air the next day.

The sun melted the sharp corners of my grief so I comfortably lived alongside it, and I think the physical activity helped me find elusive sleep. My healing had begun.

Yours will too.

You will grieve, but your grief will turn to joy.

—JOHN 16:20

35

What I've Learned So Far

There's a fine edge to new grief,
it severs nerves, disconnects reality—there's
mercy in a sharp blade. Only with time, as the
edge wears, does the real ache begin.

—CHRISTOPHER MOORE

Kids don't have much of a choice in the actions of their lives. They are required to go to school, have to learn, must pass. In the end, they discover it was all for their good, and they emerge as (hopefully) mature adults with a career path and a good life.

On this grief journey, you and I can't make many choices, either. A wise person stated it well: *you can't go around, under or over grief. You have to go through it.* Your only choice is whether to face it now or deny loss happened. Whether you want to accept reality or not, you will face grief at some point. And that part about it being all for the good in the end (*And we know that in all things God works for the good of those who love him, Romans 8:28*), well, I confess I'm still waiting. I still have my doubts.

Loss comes with accompanying lessons. I didn't want to learn them when I faced the death of my husband of nearly 47 years. Even months later I didn't want to acknowledge them. I'm stubborn that way. Regardless of my wishes, the lessons need to be learned.

Here are my top ten in no particular order.

1. Grief is painful. It goes to bed with you, wakes you umpteen times in the night, and greets you when you rise in the morning as exhausted as when you laid down the night before.

2. Grief is relentless. Reminders are everywhere. When you travel, they are in your mind, a slideshow in your head. If you stay at home, they are physical—a photo, a favorite scarf, writing found in a folder, a memento of a baseball team . . . and so much more.

3. You can't concentrate. On anything. Ever. Movies, books, lists, conversations, everyday tasks—none of them make sense. Consequently, holding a decent conversation is impossible. What's the point? Why would you want to? Nothing matters anyway. The

world is spinning, and you can barely hold on.

4. People will tell you what you should do, how you should feel, and how long grief will take. Don't believe a word they say. This is your journey meant to be taken at your pace.

5. Your friends say to call them when you want to go out, or talk, or whatever. It's impossible. You are unable to dial a phone, send a text, or communicate via email. At the worst of times, when you need companionship most, your capability to make a call is at zero. Having a bad day? Good luck. Because your hands may as well be tied behind your back and your mouth gagged. *Wow, don't I sound cynical? But read on and maybe that will change. . . .*

6. You don't remember if you ate breakfast. Or lunch. Or dinner. Your appetite has fled, and nothing sounds good. For some people the opposite is true, and they eat their way through grief. I did the first.

7. When things go wrong, as many, many things did for me in the first months, making intelligent decisions is next to impossible. Can I trust my judgment? Am I capable of making decisions? Since I can't call people, (see #5) I must figure out what to

do on my own. But I'm not rational. Hence, the decision-making process is a logical disaster.

8. Supersensitivity to nearly everything is the order of the day. The least little thing brings on the tears.

9. Depression becomes a companion on the grief journey. Oh, it may not seem to be there, but it rears its ugly head in many ways. The struggle is in the leaving it behind, not allowing the sadness to catch back up to you. And that's exhausting, too.

10. Everything is so very *hard*. Things which used to be easy are now incredibly difficult. Small challenges become enormous. You are insecure about the smallest responsibilities. It's a mountain, a very steep, very tall mountain. And all this makes you angry. Okay, fine, I lied. There are eleven things . . . forgive me, it's hard to focus. (See # 3.)

11. Holidays and special days such as birthdays are . . . well, *not fun* would be an understatement. Still, they have to be faced and endured. This is where family members and friends can help so much just by showing up and acknowledging the pain and loss. No words are necessary. You need their presence, their arms around you, their love.

Those are the most important lessons I've learned, but I here are a couple of side notes to add.

You rely on those around you to help you regain your sanity, your sense of normal (albeit a new normal), your joy. I am so grateful for my family and the friends who call, come, invite me out, text, email, pray for me, send notes and just *love* me. Their hugs and encouragement mean the world. Let people in. Allow hugs. Be open to attention. Let people give the gift of caring.

Then there's faith—I hope you have that to hang on to. I did, and it kept me sane. God kept me sane regardless of how angry I was at him. Even through the challenges I mentioned above, I'm getting through, thankful for the blessings I'm finding along the way. No, life didn't go my way. I remind myself all is going to be okay. God's in control, and that's all I need to know.

He's given me the gift of grace.

> *My grace is sufficient for you, for my*
> *power is made perfect in weakness.*
>
> —II Corinthians 12:9

36

Loneliness

*It's like I have this large black hole in my brain
and it's sucking the life out of me. The answers
are in there so I sit for hours and stare. No matter
how hard and long I look, I only see darkness.*

—Katie McGarry, Pushing the Limits

Christmas, 2014

Here it is, another Christmas week, my second one after Mel died. The twinkling lights everywhere lend a magical aspect to the season, even though we are missing snow this year and warmer temperatures make it seem more like fall. Christmas music streams in all the stores, faces wear various expressions ranging from joy and excitement to stress and exhaustion, and greetings range from 'Happy Holidays' to 'Merry Christmas.'

My trees are up and lit whenever I'm at home; the

lights are tiny sparks pinpointed randomly all over the boughs. Under the lower branches, a riotous mix of paper and ribbon cover the gifts thoughtfully purchased for children, grandchildren, and friends. All is calm in my home.

But that's the problem. Unless I have music or the TV on, it's very, very calm. Quiet. A much-too-silent night.

These days I often think of my father, a widower for twenty years. He didn't speak much of his experiences after Mom died. He bore the burden quietly, rarely talking about the loss. When he did mention it, he simply said, "it's lonely without Mom."

I thought I knew what he meant. I thought I understood. Maybe I did to a small degree, but the depth of those few words didn't impact me until March of 2013 when I experienced loss firsthand. I realize now why he seldom talked about his loneliness, why instead he carried on his life, such as it was, and said little about the condition of his hurting heart.

I love Christmas—always have. The music, the tree, the house adorned with lights and boughs of evergreen, the gifts I can't wait to give to those I love, the gatherings with close friends, and best of all the family time with all my kids and grandkids. There is a hope that is innate to Christmas, a peace in the pondering of an incomparable night when the angels told shepherds they were about to meet the Savior of the world.

I love to imagine it, seeing the sky filled with a host of heavenly beings, all proclaiming the miracle of a baby in a manger.

Amazing.

And yet I am incredibly sad. Some of the joy of the season is gone, some of the wonder is diminished, and part of my heart is so very heavy. As my dad said, at the end of the day, it's lonely.

Sadness, loneliness, fatigue—these are all normal parts of the grief journey you are on. Be encouraged, though. God understands every emotion, every thought. He hears every cry of your heart.

> *But you, O Lord, be not far off;*
> *O my strength, come quickly to help me.*

—PSALM 22:19

Cold Season

Wintertime comes
Deep snow buries memories
Cold winds scatter life's detritus
Chills permeate bones

Frost paints windowsills
Snowflake art ices windows
In vain, fire blazes, tries to
Chase the chill of absence

Nothing coaxes sunshine
Nothing melts the ice
Caking on a doorsill
Crossed by no one

Wintertime has come
No chance of warmth for bones
The blizzard swells and grows
Drifts over the road of memory

Where are the paths to summer?
Why won't cold seasons die
Like the ghost once in my mind?
Where has he gone?

37

It's Not All About Me—Anymore

Even if happiness forgets you a little bit,
never completely forget about it.

—Jacques Prévert

I was the focus of attention for a while, and there was a strange juxtaposition of being what I needed, physically, emotionally and spiritually, and what I selfishly expected. In many ways you become like a child when grief descends. Unable to make a meal, read a book, compile a grocery list, choose what to wear, or handle even the simplest of tasks like answering a phone, there is comfort in letting other people take the calls. You are grieving, trying to keep going, trying in vain to sleep.

Those first two weeks my daughter filled the role I couldn't. Her help, companionship and uncanny intuition of what I needed, gave me comfort. I functioned like a ghost, wandering without purpose through the house while she cooked meals, did wash, cleaned up dishes, fielded calls and gently steered me to bed at the end of the day. She suggested we go downstairs to watch the whole first season of Downton Abbey on Netflix. We turned on the gas fireplace, snuggled under an afghan and ate dark chocolate sea salt caramels as the episodes unfolded and we lost ourselves in the story.

My sons would call to check in, visit, reassure me they were there for me. They helped when they could with things around the house. I knew I could depend on them for support and understanding. Marc came as often as feasible from Milwaukee. Jeff stopped by to check on me, see if I needed anything, and to give me a hug. All of them told me so many times how much they love me. What a blessing.

People called, they sent cards, so very many cards. They came in droves bringing soup, casseroles, baked goods, books on grief, hugs, condolences.

Here's the thing, though. At some point the outpouring had to end. My daughter went home. People stopped visiting. The phone stopped ringing, and the cards stopped coming. Life went on for everyone around me. My kids had jobs, families, their lives to get on with, as they should. Friends had their issues, their lives to run.

And I felt stranded.

We arrive at a point when we have to stop using the *I'm a widow* card and suck it up. As hard as it may be, we who have experienced loss need to watch for that moment.

Can I give you a definite time when you have to stop? The short answer is no; I cannot. Again, every person, every circumstance differs. But pay attention, watch for it; you'll know. A little twinge of conscience will tell you.

Once you've reached that point, lean on God. Your friends and family have done their job, but God is never finished helping, sustaining, watching over and blessing you. Isn't that just the best news ever?

So go forth in joy.

> *Weeping may remain for a night,*
> *but rejoicing comes in the morning.*

—PSALM 30:5B

38

Joy In The Midst Of Grief

Sorrows come to stretch out
places in the heart for joy.

— EDWIN MARKHAM

The last sentence on the previous page about going forth in joy—did it catch you off guard? Have you noticed I've used the word 'joy' throughout these chapters? How can grief and joy coexist, you ask? Sounds impossible. Most of us hear the word 'joy' and think of happiness, fun, lightheartedness, celebration. Our culture gives a different meaning to a word never meant to mean happy. We hear it in Christmas carols (*Joy to the World*), read it in books (she jumped for joy) and we wonder. Can you feel grief and joy at the same time?

Many years ago I attended a Bible study for women on the fruit of the Spirit, such as love, peace, patience, *joy*. Our leader, Betsy, described a time when her oldest son was aboard a ship and in dangerous waters during the Bay of Pigs incident. She had no way of knowing if he was alive or dead or captured or injured or safe. She and her husband were worried, scared, and afraid of what they might hear from the armed forces.

Still, she told us, she had joy in her heart. We all looked at each other. Worry, fear, anxiety and ... *joy*?

Joy, she explained, isn't a feeling of happiness. It is a sense of peace, contentment, confidence in a greater being. A knowing that whatever happens, and whatever circumstances you find yourself in, God is in control. Did you get that? GOD is in control. Does this mean Betsy and her family weren't worried about their son? Of course not. They feared for his life, knew he might not come home again. In spite of this Betsy reaffirmed her belief God is in control. Not you, not me, not some random person. God. It's His responsibility, not ours. He brought Betsy's son home, safe and unharmed months later.

Knowing you can't change a thing without His help, you can rest easy. God had control of that situation. No matter how things turn out, He's got your back. He's got this situation. Allow Him to carry you now, in your grief.

Joy. Such a small word. Such an incredible message. Take time to experience it. Joy in all circumstances at all times, *no matter what*.

Give thanks to the Lord, for he is good;
his love endures forever.

—PSALM 118:1

39

The Blessing Of Friendship

The friend who can be silent with us
in a moment of confusion or despair, who can
stay with us in an hour of grief and bereavement,
who can tolerate not knowing . . . not healing . . .
not curing . . . that is a friend indeed.

—HENRI NOUWEN

I don't know why God gave me such wonderful friends, but without them I would not have made it through the remainder of 2013 and into 2014. Though I've had difficult years in my life, that one was the hardest. Nothing could have prepared me for or prevented me from experiencing the events of those months.

I'm blessed with a beautiful mix of friends from many different areas of my life. Some I haven't seen since high school, some I seldom see but are friends on Facebook, while others live in the area but lead busy lives and may not connect very often. Many are at the ready on a daily basis.

The thing about friends, though, at least the real ones, is that time, distance, frequency of communication—none of that matters. When I need them, they come. They send notes, call, give me hugs, take me for dinner, invite me to a movie or the theater, show concern in a million little ways that warm my heart and would make Mel proud. They love the messy, complicated, sometimes unhinged me.

This is my truth: God placed people in my life at exactly the spot where I need them. Each has their role to play, their perfect way of supporting me. No one person is more important than another. Every single one of them has given me a gift I can never repay. They have shown me *love*. The love of God personified.

How blessed I am. I hope, you are also.

Thank you, Lord, for the incredible gift of friends who hold me up when I can't stand on my own.

40

Growth

*Hope . . . sometimes that's all you
have when you have nothing else. If
you have it, you have everything.*

—UNKNOWN

Ever think about how a flower begins its life? First, the seemingly dead seed needs to be planted in the ground to sprout. As the soil and water nurture it, the seed splits, exposing a green interior which produces a stem. That stem must push up through the soil to get the sunlight needed to sustain life. Sometimes, amazingly, it pushes up through asphalt. At the same time the stem grows toward light, roots need to struggle downward to establish an anchor which will hold the plant in place and prevent wind and rain from knocking it over.

Sounds hard, like a lot of work. And painful. And

time-consuming. That seed has to have relentless determination. It has to break out of the darkness of the shell covering it in order to grow. You've seen it, the weed breaking through cement to bask in the sun.

The seed of hope has just as hard a job. It needs a place to be planted, an environment in which to flourish. If it isn't nurtured, the seed will die before it has a chance to begin to grow. True, for a while there seems to be no hope for a normal life. You are in a darkness that can't be penetrated by light of any kind. But that will change over time if you allow it. We all have the means to propagate the growth of hope. The sun and water a plant needs is comparable to the openness hope needs us to provide. We have to let it happen regardless of the pain. We have to let air and space in by talking about our loss, giving the pain free reign to wash over us, and being willing to mourn in any way we need to mourn.

Over the months, I've had to accept that sometimes I will cry in public for no apparent reason, in front of a variety of people. It's okay. Grief is nothing to be ashamed of. The bonus is, once in a while your story will resonate with another person who has experienced a similar loss.

Not long ago I was speaking with someone I had just met. She mentioned that her son had died two years before. Her tears were right at the surface, and I assured her it was okay to cry. She told me her story; he had passed at the age of 28 under tragic circumstances. I, in turn, shared my loss with her, and when she was leaving, she turned and opened her arms to me. That hug was so warm and comforting because we shared a common story—our grief may have been completely different, but we each understood the pain of loss. Both of us felt richer from the experience of sharing.

As she left, we agreed that it was good to talk about her son and my husband with each other. In some ways, sharing gives hope and helps dull the edges. We need to know we are not alone on this journey of grief.

You are not alone. You and I are part of a community.

Deposits of unfinished grief reside in
more American hearts than I ever imagined.
Until these pockets are opened and their contents
aired openly, they block unimagined amounts of
human growth and potential. They can give rise to
bizarre and unexplained behavior which
causes untold internal stress.

—ROBERT KAVANAUGH

41

What You Need To Know

I wish someone would have told me what
to say and do for a new widow or widower. I hope
I will be a more compassionate friend.

—ANNONYMOUS

The last thing any of us wants is to hurt a grieving person, and yet we do it in many ways without realizing it. I cringe to think of the clichés I've used and the things I've said that sent arrows of pain through the heart of the very person I'm trying to comfort.

There are things you should (or should not) say to, or do for, someone who has experienced a loss, and though a few of the most important ones are mentioned in this chapter, there are more if you simply pay attention. Awareness of these dos and don'ts can avoid causing pain to a bereaved person.

• Don't tell someone who has lost a loved one to be

thankful they had the person in their life for as long as they did. At the moment of loss all they want is to have the person back.

- Don't say the deceased is in a better place. In that fog called grief the better place is beside them, not up in heaven.

- Don't compare their loss with that of someone else. This is their pain, and it needs to be acknowledged, not diminished by comparison.

- And never, never, ever tell them, "I know how you feel." You don't. You can't. Every situation is different, every relationship has its complications. This is *their* pain.

- Don't say, "Call and let me know what I can do for you." Although this is a wonderful idea, there's a problem. In the time of grief your memory goes on hiatus. I had many people say that to me, but by the end of the day, I wasn't able to remember who they were or what they offered. Because a lot of people say that. A better comment might be, "In a few days I'll call you to see how I can help."

- Instead of asking when would they like a meal, be

specific. "I'm making spaghetti for dinner tonight and there's extra. May I bring some over to you at six?" Or, "I have a couple of hours free this afternoon. I'd like to help with cleaning or washing clothes. Would two o'clock be a good time?"

You can fill in the blanks, but be clear what you would like to do. Maybe there is gardening to be done, grocery shopping, snow shoveling, window washing. But with any of these offers it would be wise to wait a few weeks. A couple of months after the loss the offer of a meal or other help is a reminder to the widow that you remember her. By then other people have stopped helping.

"What can I do for you?" is a question that puts a lot of burden on the bereaved. They can barely breathe or get from one day to the next, let alone try to think about how others can help. In that first year or two, be specific. Stop in to offer a hug. Call and invite the widower for coffee or lunch. Be there.

Just show up. Keep showing up. That's the biggest thing you can do.

There's something else few people realize. The common perception is after a year, maybe two, grief magically disappears. If only that were true. Grief doesn't end, and there are moments when the pain is just as raw four or six or ten years later as it was in the weeks following the loss. So that part about just showing up? That's even more important as time goes on. Remember those things that needed doing right after a major loss? They still need doing. Those hugs, the notes saying thoughts are being sent, the spontaneous calls, the dropping by, are even more important and welcomed as time goes on.

When a puzzle piece is missing, the picture is incomplete. It will never be right, never look whole again, no matter how long you leave it on your table. The piece is gone, the puzzle isn't the same, can't be the same. So is the life of someone grieving a loss. There will always be an empty space.

Missing someone is your heart's way
of reminding you that you love them.

—ANONYMOUS

42

On The Way Home

*My grief journey has no one destination.
I will not "get over it." The understanding that I
don't have to be done is liberating. I will mourn
this death for the rest of my life.*

—Alan D. Wolfelt, The Wilderness of Grief

The title for this book has a double meaning. Mel was out running, heading back home on the day he entered heaven. Instead of coming to his earthly home, he was ushered into the clouds to his heavenly home on that day. What a welcome must have awaited him!

I have to admit I am thankful he was taken quickly and with a minimum of pain. He often spoke of his fear that he would linger when his time came, that he would spend years in a nursing facility, suffer a long and painful death. For him, this way of dying was a blessing. It would have been painful to watch him suffer, but I also confess that, for a long time, I was angry I didn't get to say goodbye.

I don't know what's more difficult. Sudden death is a shock, but prolonged dying is hard on the person dying and the family having to witness suffering. Neither is easy.

Sometimes words put into poetic form have a deeper meaning than prose. I found it comforting to express my thoughts in poetic form shortly after my husband died. I have interspersed a few of my poems throughout this book to correspond with relevant chapters.

So where am I on this journey today? Though I've navigated the firsts and seconds and more, I am well aware the hard days aren't over. I don't know what's in store for me in the future. I don't know when or if things will get easier. I do know I will never get over Mel's death. I also know I will learn how to live with it. It will exist alongside me, gradually becoming a companion as the pain it brings lessens.

I know grief will never go away.

But here's the thing. I've learned how resilient the human spirit can be. Some days are so incredibly hard they just can't end soon enough. Other days are beautiful, filled with hope and joy. Regardless of what I face when I awaken, each day is another chance to do things right. And isn't that all we can ask for? To do things right. Alone or side-by-side with someone dear to us. With anger or with love. With frustration or determination. Whether we like our situation or not.

Try this. Each day, before you go to sleep, think of at least one thing that brought you joy during the day. A pretty flower, an unexpected phone call, a fresh breeze. When you wake in the morning, thank God for another day, another chance to find beauty and meaning. Nurture your resilience, turn your focus on the gifts you have. And be loving and gentle toward those newly enmeshed in grief.

Give thanks in every circumstance. . . . *Thank you, Lord. For everything.*

May God richly bless you with His comfort and peace as you walk this uncharted path.

And we know that in all things God
works for the good of those who love him, who
have been called according to his purpose.

—ROMANS 8:28

Acknowledgements

The word lovingkindness has the power to change the world. I have been blessed to learn the true meaning of that word, because over the past four years it has been rained down on me by the most incredible people on the planet.

There are so many to thank. My early encouragers, the Cool Kids; Joe Roper, Kelly O'Dell Stanley, Irene Fridsma, Dan Johnson, Sarah Schmidt, Kelsey Timmerman, Lisa Rice Wheeler, and most recently Marcia Kendall, you all had my back through the darkest days of my life, and you challenged me to share those days. My very dear friend and possibly the sweetest person I've ever known, the heart of the Midwest Writers Conference, Jama Kehoe Bigger, whose hugs cannot be matched. My Tribe, whose arms were wrapped around me at every possible moment and whose gentle prodding made this book a reality; Irene Fridsma, Mary Bartman and AnnMary Dykstra. My sweet friends who fed me, took me out, had me over, invited me to movies, and showed the love of God in ways too numerous to mention, especially George and Lynn Sullivan and Bruce and Lynnel Huizen. How blessed I am to have you and so many others in my life.

My family, with whom I walked this path, and without whom I would have fallen into despair; Marc and Brittany DeVries, you have loved me through the hardest days even though distance has kept you from being present all the time. Michele and Ronn Smith, your love, support and prayers held me up when I could not stand on my own. Jeff and Brooke DeVries, you reminded me that, while this loss was immeasurable, life has many wonders to gift to us.

To my beautiful grandchildren; Hannah, who excels in so many ways, has leadership qualities that will serve her well in college and beyond, and is beautiful both inside and out. Paige, whose sense of fun draws others to her and who is growing into a lovely young woman, Micah, who has a smile that lights up a room, and who loves soccer like his grandpa did. Josie, whose sense of humor and love for the dramatic brings so much life into the family, and who looks more like her beautiful mom every day, and Xander, whose love for learning has him pushing way beyond his grade level, and who plays a mean game of soccer in the fall and baseball in the spring. Grandpa would have loved seeing these precious children become the amazing young people they are. Each of these family members are my heart, reminding me daily what family means.

A special thanks to Kelly O'Dell Stanley and Irene Fridsma, my early readers who helped shape this book with valuable input and suggestions. My deepest gratitude to my boy Joe Roper, whose help with all the logistics of layout, formatting and expert advice in getting this book into ebook form as well as published into a professional looking paperback made the process so much easier. To Kelly O'Dell Stanley who used her graphic design talents to make a beautiful cover.

To all those I have mentioned and so many, many more, thank you for your love, support, tender care, strength and concern in the darkest times. Each of you has made this journey less lonely. And above all, my thanks to the God of Angel Armies who has carried me through the most impossible days. I am truly blessed.

Made in the USA
Lexington, KY
01 July 2017